Typewriters, Bombs, Jellyfish

Typewriters, Bombs, Jellyfish

Essays

TOM McCARTHY

 New York Review Books New York

This is a New York Review Book

published by The New York Review of Books

435 Hudson Street, New York, NY 10014

www.nyrb.com

Copyright © 2017 by Tom McCarthy
All rights reserved.

A catalog record for this book is available from The Library of Congress.

ISBN 978-1-68137-086-6
Also available as an electronic book; ISBN 978-1-68137-087-3

Printed in the United States of America on acid-free paper

1 3 5 7 9 10 8 6 4 2

Contents

For all my
New York friends

Introduction
The Coming Goo

I RECALL READING, in *The New York Review of Books* a couple of years ago, an article that said jellyfish were taking over the planet. Reviewing a study by marine biologist Lisa-ann Gershwin, the piece pointed to instances of giant agglomerations of the things covering (or saturating) ocean stretches up to sixty miles long, destroying fisheries, clogging up the intake-vents of shoreline factories; when, in 1999, they blocked the cooling system of a Filipino power plant, causing a blackout, it was presumed—and widely reported—that there'd been a coup. Invertebrate guerrillas, plasmic terrorists. Last year, Donna Haraway published an essay on "Tentacular Thinking" in *e-flux*, calling for fibrous, flagellated, tendriled, and microbial revolt, accompanied by an agitprop poster showing invertebrates—"the 97%" (of animal diversity)—marching beneath the banner "Octopi Wall Street." This is funny, and sharp; but Gershwin's cnidarian revolutionaries are more sexy, because they're more brazenly militaristic: they even once apparently took on—and beat—the nuclear warship *USS Ronald Reagan*, subduing it not with thrashing and encoiling arms out of Jules Verne but through an older, Coleridgean tactic of softly yet ineluctably sludging it fast within a sea that had become pure slime.

These essays were written between 2002 and 2016. Some were commissioned as introductions to reissued novels; some as articles; some as live lectures; one as a BBC radio performance. You launch them, and they float around for a while, catching and refracting various types of light; then this same translucence camouflages them against the general background, and they fade from view. But they're still there, trailing strands in all directions, looking—seductively, or with toxic malevolence, or both—for points of contact, larger cluster-meshes to lace into, feed off, and recalibrate, or just to sting. Sometimes they break down as clumps of them detach and, like in *Terminator 2*, run into other clumps, and something starts reconstituting that might or might not be what was there before. Eventually, you realize that a kind of saturation level has been reached; there's a critical mass of goo in circulation; and it's coming back, lodging, sticking...

Does this mass have intent? Is it governed by some kind of plan? A systematic, or at least strategic (revolutionary? or reactionary?) program? What citadel or intake-vent is it storming? Even if it lacks the central nervous system that would enable it to *think* it had a plan, could one be attributed to it retrospectively, or vicariously, or by default? Maybe, maybe not. The only way of beginning to answer these questions is to scoop these essays up and float them out again, as one big cluster.

I'M EXTREMELY GRATEFUL to Melanie Jackson and Edwin Frank, without whom this collection would never have taken shape. Also to Ed Ruscha, for allowing me to use his beautiful image on the cover. And to Jonathan Pegg, and the many collaborators—institutional, commercial, and (perhaps most importantly) amical—whose kindness has allowed the pieces such a hospitable environment in which to spawn and multiply.

Meteomedia, or Why London's Weather Is in the Middle of Everything

I LIVE IN a twelfth-floor Central London flat. The flat has long, tall windows facing west and north. Talking to people on the phone, I stare across the city and the sky. The vista usually provides a backdrop to the conversation. Often, though, it's the conversation's subject: I tell friends what weather they will have in twenty minutes, warning those in Hackney that long, vertical walls of rain are gliding towards them over Islington and Dalston, or assuring those caught in a West End shower that the broad shafts of sunlight I can see sweeping northwards from Big Ben will hit them soon. During public events—jubilee fly-pasts, test matches, May Day demonstrations—the television becomes a shared chart or crib sheet: I can reference the blimp or helicopter that I know is on my interlocutor's screen as well as mine and tell him or her that two hundred feet to its east the cloud that's worrying the umpire's light meter gives over to blue skies in St. John's Wood, or that the rioters and police we're watching battling it out in Oxford Street will shortly be united by a drenching.

Weather and communication: that is the two-fold promise modern London's airspace makes. Aerials and phone-masts pick up, decode, encode and transmit again through clouds that swallow and regurgitate them or slide by above them scanning roofs and streets like barcode. When viewed from high up, London invites commentary, interpretation and prognosis—more so than other cities due to its ever-changing climate. Weather and communication, weather and telecommunication: the tallest (and hence most weather-enveloped) building visible from my flat is the British Telecom Tower. Although built a decade and a half before 1979 (and christened the Post Office Tower), the building owes its present name and status to that year's election and its aftermath. In 1981 Margaret Thatcher's government separated BT from the Post Office; in 1984 they floated BT as a PLC, selling 50.2 percent of its shares to the public. Throughout the eighties, though, and to the present day, the Tower has remained closed to the same public who own it. Technically, the Tower is what is known as a Pulse Code Modulation (PCM) Switching Center—one of the world's very first. Staring at it day in and day out, month after month as it lights up, looms out of fog, bounces sunlight, dodges lightning and gets drubbed by hail, I like to fantasize that in its upper floors sit gods, or at least priests, who modulate all of the city's sky's flows, who set its pulse-rate, write its code and flip its switches. When London is studied centuries from now by alien terrologists, this building and not Saint Paul's will be identified as its religious heart, its spire.

Weather, communication, code, interpretation, influence: these things have always gone together. For both Seneca and Aristotle, the airy region was a region of conveyance, of transferral and translation, in which "meteors" or atmospheric phenomena (*meteor* means "elevated," "lofty" or "sublime") were produced by the influence of the celestial sphere on the sublunary one. For Virgil, too, weather told a coded tale of influence, of cause and effect, and hence was decryptable: his *Georgics* describes a world of signs in which the movement of ants, swallows, frogs, and ravens can be read and interpreted, as can the appearance of the clouds, sun and moon. Seventeenth-century English Puritans treated the sky as a switchboard connecting them to God, divining portents in its storms and lightshows. The anonymous author of the 1641 text *A Strange Wonder, or, The Cities Amazement* (subtitled *News from Heaven*) describes exceptional meteorological events as God's "signes and Tokens," "prodigious ensignes," "ominous harbingers," "Cyphers," "notable Messengers." Londoners were so addicted to such Cyphers that, according to Defoe, during the plague years they scoured the clouds constantly for "shapes and figures, representations and appearances." It's standard to think of the atmosphere as a medium, a "pervading or enveloping substance" (indeed, the terms "air," "ether," and "environment" all appear in the *Oxford English Dictionary*'s definition of the word *medium*), but we should go further. Weather is, and always has been, more than just a medium: it is also *media*.

Shakespeare understood this. In *The Tempest*, that great play about the weather, Caliban tells Trinculo and Stephano that the island's atmosphere is "full of noises, sounds and sweet airs," the humming of "a thousand twangling instruments" and "voices." He could be describing radio. Caliban is not so much consuming and decoding these transmissions as feeling them billow around him, finding form and losing it again, like clouds. The weather is a teaser. "Weather writes, erases and rewrites itself upon the sky with the endless fluidity of language; and it is with language that we have sought throughout history to apprehend it," writes Richard Hamblyn in *The Invention of Clouds*. Easier said than done, though. Aristotle knew that *epagoge*, or linguistic reasoning, would never yield meteorological certainty; the best it offers us is speculation. Vladimir Janković, author of *Reading the Skies: A Cultural History of English Weather*, points out that since *meteoros*, "rising," can refer to rising wind within the stomach, *meteoro-logeo* means not only "talk of high things" but also "windy speech," "high talk," "empty musings." Shakespeare understood this too, as Hamlet's ability to make the verbose Polonius see in the same cloud a whale, a weasel and a camel testifies. Hamlet's deliberate mobilization of language's powers of indeterminacy is linked to weather throughout: "when the wind is southerly I know a hawk from a handsaw," he claims—an utterance that Claudius's spies and twentieth-century critics alike will busy themselves trying, and failing, to decipher.

When language grapples with the weather there is slippage and there is displacement. Johnson's quip that "when two Englishmen meet, their first talk is of the weather" is an easy one to make; Gwendolen's intuition (in Wilde's *The Importance of Being Earnest*) that "whenever people talk about the weather, I always feel quite certain that they mean something else" is much more astute. For centuries manuals and charts have tried to map meteorological phenomena onto social ones, from *The English Chapmans and Travellers Almanack for the Year of Christ 1697* (which aligns the ten-week frost with the gunpowder plot, the time when "the whole heaven seemed to burn with fire" with the invention of the art of printing) to Election Weather Tables compiled by today's Met Office (Labour only wins in fair weather, apparently; that fateful day in 1979 was foul) or the Weather-to-Stock Market Correspondence Graphs studied by the more esoteric among our economists. The weather unfolds endlessly across non-meteorological discourses, across Other Stuff. It's an index both of truth and of all that's random, meaningless. Like all media, it bears a plethora of messages—perhaps even *the* message—while simultaneously supplying no more than conversational, neutral, white noise.

LYING ALMOST EXACTLY on the line that runs between my windows and the British Telecom Tower is the London Weather Centre. It's been there, on Clerkenwell Road, since 1992. In 1996, one year before the weather-change that would reverse/consolidate (delete as you deem appropriate) the political winds blowing since 1979, its parent institution, the Met Office, went down the same road as BT had twelve years previously and became a trading fund. A digital and free-market analogue to the Mount Pleasant postal depot round the corner, the London Weather Centre acts as a big sorting office, receiving, separating, ordering and redirecting meteorological information that's come in from all around the country and the world, tailoring it to suit various clients' needs. So football stadia in Sunderland and Portsmouth, aerodromes in Glasgow, electricity and gas stations in Anglesey and Norfolk all receive prognostic bulletins from the London Weather Centre—even if the source-data behind those bulletins was gathered not two miles from the stadium, aerodrome or station. It's only official weather-data if it's passed through London. This pattern stretches back four hundred years. With the explosion in the seventeenth century of a new, popular, cheap-to-produce media form, the pamphlet, people started sending in to London endless weather reports. They had great titles: *A Report from Abbingdon towne in Berkshire, being a relation of what harme Thunder and Lightning did on Thursday last upon the body of Humphrey Richardson, a rich miserable farmer. With Exhortation for England to repent*; or *A Full and True Relation of the Strange and Wonderful Apparitions which were Seen in the Clouds upon Tuesday Evening at Seven of the Clock.* Why did their authors send them here? Because they craved inclusion in the next issue of *Philosophical Transactions*, the journal of the London-based Royal Society. Being reprinted there made the texts "official" and "legitimate," conferring what Janković calls "visibility within the national republic of letters."

Initially, these reports were event-based, for the good reason that weather was conceived not as a system but rather as a set of discrete occurrences. By the mid-seventeenth century word had reached London of the Italian stage designer Giacomo Torelli's magnificent, multi-canopied cloud-sets, in which rolls of painted cumulus were lowered and raised by ropes and pulleys: the real weather, too, was thought of in spectacular, theatrical terms. Edward Ward describes in *British Wonders* the "scene" in which "strange coruscations in the skies" appeared "whilst crowds and mortals stood below beholding the tremendous show." When the Thames froze, the weather-show was augmented by human spectacles: archery contests, skating, games of football, acrobatics. In the late eighteenth century, when hygrometry, barometry and electro-chemical research took over, lecturers would show off their gizmos to audiences who cheered in admiration as these new Torellis reproduced clouds, lightning and tides inside glass boxes. By the nineteenth century, *Philosophical Transactions* carried titles such as *On the late Extraordinary Depression of the Barometer* and provincial correspondents gave over to London-based professionals processing readings telegraphed to them by armies of data gatherers.

A more fundamental shift than that from the anecdotal to the scientific, though, was the shift from an event-logic to an event-*space* logic in the thinking of weather. This, too, occurred in London—and it happened as a media event,

took me there to show me the Stevenson Screen, rain gauge and Campbell-Stokes sunshine recorder (a crystal ball with a metal ellipse around it)—but most of all he took me there to see the view. I've never had such a strong sense of being in the middle of everything. You could see St. Paul's, the Wheel, the Telecom Tower, King's Cross, my flat. You could see Hampstead Heath. You could see all the way to the Crystal Palace and the Alexandra Palace pylons, London's city gates. Contemporary London does have gates: the edges of its broadcast zones and weather zones. Just as London has its own TV and radio, it has its own weather. Snow on the roof of a car driving through town on a cold-but-not-arctic winter's day designates a hick, or at least one of those semi-hicks, 0208-ers. The city's buildings generate their own heat and redirect the wind, creating gale-filled corridors and doldrums within feet of one another. Peter Ackroyd describes how London's smog was so bad in the fifties that its theatres' audiences couldn't see the actors. It's Torelli all over again—but this time with the city playing the role of the creative genius. London can make rain fall upwards. It pulls off remarkable, stupendous atmospheric tricks thanks to its energy, its density, its lovely, lovely pollution. On some evenings I'll phone or be phoned by one of two or three friends who also live high up, my fellow meta-metropolitans, and we'll watch cloud-strips and vapor-trails alike light up and glow, hit from below by a sun drowning in haze behind the Telecom Tower. The colors are unnatural—blood-orange, purple, RGB—and constantly changing, often making us quite literally shout out in amazement, sometimes even moving us to tears.

THE DRAMATIC ATMOSPHERE, or atmospheric drama, of contemporary London is like that of Troy: it is the drama of a city under siege. London has always thought of itself as besieged—by the Black Death, by Holland's Fleet, by foreign speculators. And these phantoms have always ridden with the weather. Winds carried plague-spoors and bore Dutch ships towards us ("Catholic Winds," as they were known). The great stock market crash of 1987, in which BT's shares crashed to earth alongside the freemarket promises of 1979, coincided (as those esoteric graph-compiling economists will point out) with a hurricane. That was exceptional, though: London's weather, generally, is what climate statisticians call "median": middling, not extreme. The city doesn't get tornadoes or typhoons. It does, however, face one major meteorological threat: flood. Strong tides racing up the Thames have caused disastrous inundation several times, even sweeping London Bridge away in 1090. These floods continued well into the twentieth century, but were put on hold with the completion, in 1984, of the Thames Barrier just beyond Greenwich. I grew up in Greenwich while the Barrier was being built. On our classroom walls in the late seventies were posters showing a child's doll floating over a submerged street; from time to time slow wails would fill the air as flood sirens were tested; in the night I'd picture the doll's eyes as I drifted into sleep to the sound of piledrivers hammering steel beams into the riverbed, a constant Morse-code pulse that spelled out "danger." Now, less than two decades after its completion, the Thames Barrier faces imminent obsolescence due to rising global water levels and the increasing downward tilting of England's South East. According to Alex Hill, the Hadley Center's most extreme end prediction (modern science, like classical poetry or Puritan theology, has its own narratives of disaster: ozone depletion, global warming, acid rain) is for Cambridge to have a beach by 2050. The night after Hill told me that, I had another vision as I fell asleep: a small Dutch boy with Johnny Rotten's face pulling his finger from a dam and smiling as he flashed his maniacal eyes, two gleaming white chrysanthemums made of ivory or marble. As Rilke said, every angel is terrifying.

London is a great city and, like all great cities, it is haunted by the specter of its ruin. An apocalyptic atmosphere broods over it, one registered in the work of the great writers who have taken London on, from Pepys to Pynchon—and nowhere more so than in T. S. Eliot's *The Waste Land*. Published in 1922, the year the Met Office broadcast its first Radio forecast on the BBC, the poem is one long weather report: it rains in April, snows in winter, rains in summer too; the wind blows towards the *Heimat*; there is fog on London Bridge; the Thames flows out past Greenwich (where the sirens go *Weilala leia*); there's a drought, but black clouds are massing over Himavant; the thunder speaks; *datta*. In *The Waste Land*, all cities become London; London becomes all cities, cracking and bursting in the violet air as their towers tumble to the ground. The poem's privileged tense is the ongoing present: breeding, mixing, stirring, covering. This is a feature common to all weather reports. Listen out for it next time you hear the shipping forecast or watch the weather section of the news. They never use an active verb, never say "it will rain," "winds will blow": it's always "becoming windier," "clearing up," "moving westward," "growing brighter." I asked Alex Hill why this was. "Simple," he said. "You can only describe weather as being in transition from a point *A* to a point *B*. In transition *between*—never *at*." In dramatic terms, it's called *in medias res*: in the middle of things.

Since 2001, as the global climate heats up in more ways than one, London, caught at the confluence of systems moving over from the States and from the Middle East, finds itself even more *in medias res*. When storm-clouds groan and rumble, people scour the sky for airplanes flying too low. I track them from my windows, waiting for the day when one of them will hurtle like a meteor into the Telecom Tower, painting the sky a new blood-orange. If it happens it will be spectacular. Until then, we'll continue talking about the weather.

2002

Why *Ulysses* Matters

IN 2002, I wrote, with Simon Critchley, a short essay on Joyce. We delivered it at the International James Joyce Symposium—the eighteenth one, held in Trieste, the windswept Adriatic city that, depending on how you parse a certain phrase of Joyce's own, either gave him cirrhosis, turned him into an autophagic cannibal, or turned itself, through some miraculous alchemy—metempsychosis, Leopold Bloom might have called it—into the distilled body that's the subject of these new reflections:

And Trieste, ah Trieste ate I my liver!

In other words: In Trieste I ate my liver; or (after Verlaine), Trieste *était mon livre*—Trieste was, or became, my book, namely *Ulysses*. The phrase itself doesn't come from *Ulysses*; it comes from *Finnegans Wake*—but it refers in grand part to the former, points (sadly, retrospectively) toward it as *triste* Trieste did to Dublin. That seemed like a good place to start our essay, then: not Trieste but *somewhere else*. "Our hypothesis," we grandiosely stated, "is that in Joyce and elsewhere"—and we added at this point a short aside: "(where Joyce might be seen as the index for an elsewhere of absolutely modern literary, visual and musical art)..."

It's this aside that interests me right now, not the hypothesis that followed. I think we were onto something. "...the index for an elsewhere of absolutely modern literary, visual and musical art." It sounds good. What does it mean? I don't know—but I still think we were onto something. If that "something" is to be recovered, though, it needs to be untangled from a mesh of contradictions. If the modern is contingent, if modernity itself is understood as no more than a confluence of historical and political and technological and aesthetic contingencies, how could one talk about its "absolute" or non-conditional manifestation? Were we picturing some cultural thermometer whose lower end would run to minus-273, the type of absolute zero that the early Barthes ascribed to the post-Symbolists? If so, would Joyce's work stand *at* that end, or would it, still warm, merely point to it, a compass needle that will always show some other north? An "index": for the great semiotician Charles Sanders Peirce, this—the indexical—names a key dimension of the sign—of any sign, be it linguistic or mathematical; yet, as any mathematician will tell you, the "absolute" value of a number is precisely its non-indexical value. Absolutes and indices don't go together.

But all this is getting needlessly complicated, when in fact it's very simple. How do you write after *Ulysses*? That's the question. "Whenever I sit down to write a novel," Anthony Burgess claimed, "it is with a sense of despair, because I know I'll never match that book." It isn't just that Joyce writes *better* than anyone else (although he does); beyond that, it's the sense that *Ulysses*'s publication entails a kind of rapture for literature, an event in equal parts ecstatic and catastrophic—perhaps even apocalyptic. A certain naive realism is no longer possible after it; but hasn't every alternative, every avant-garde maneuver imaginable, *also* been anticipated and exhausted by it too? As though that weren't enough, Joyce returns to the scene of his own crime, arriving not incognito (in the manner of his shady non-character McIntosh), but brazenly assuming the role of principle mourner. Just as *Ulysses* was initially conceived as an extra chapter to *Dubliners*, *Finnegans Wake* gestated as a nineteenth episode of *Ulysses*. We should not only consider all three works as part of a continuum whose critical moment (and I use this term in the dramatic sense, the sense of crisis) remains *Ulysses*, but also view *Ulysses* itself as a work whose own wake, and that, perhaps, of the novel *tout court*, is already at work in it. What new patterning, what plowing

of the sea, could a writer envisage that would pattern independent of the ripple-field already sent out by Joyce's
churning-up, the sum of its mutating patterns? Derrida (as
so often) hits the nail on the head when he complains of
the *Wake*'s relentless "hypermnesia" that "a priori indebts
you, inscribes you in advance in the book you are reading."
"The future," he affirms, "is reserved in it."

DERRIDA'S COMPLAINT IS, at base, an economic one:
doubly so, with its dual metaphors of debt and of reserve.
And this was the "hypothesis" Critchley and I advanced in
Europe's former storehouse or profit-and-loss portal of Trieste: that, in Joyce, economics is elevated to the level of
cultural form. Shakespeare might reflect, in *The Merchant
of Venice*, on the moneying of love, or Flaubert in *Madame
Bovary* on the penetration and determination of all areas of
human life by capital, but in Joyce money becomes literature
itself, and vice versa. In *Finnegans Wake*, pages become
banknotes, scraps of "pecuniar interest"; the manuscript of
the debt-ridden writer Shem, another marker for the pound
or "livre" that is *Ulysses*, becomes "an epical forged cheque"
passed off "on the public for his [Shem's/Joyce's] own private

profit"; the economic aspect of the very verb *to tell* is fully played out as the book's whole tale or content becomes "retaled."

Becomes—or rather, has already become: by *Finnegans Wake*, the "economantarchy" (as Joyce calls it) that is literature's trading-floor is fully up and running. But the minting, I would argue, happens back in *Ulysses*. "The problem," Stephen tells Buck Mulligan after the latter scolds him for trying to trade Shakespearian theory for a bit of English coin in Chapter One, "is to get money." Should they solicit this, he sarcastically inquires, from Haines or from the milkwoman who's just passed by? The latter takes money from them and extends them credit at the same time—but her real-terms contribution (as economists would say) to the novel is the stunning short speech that she delivers:

> —Bill, sir? she said, halting. Well, it's seven mornings a pint at twopence is seven twos is a shilling and twopence over and these three mornings a quart at fourpence is three quarts is a shilling. That's a shilling and one and two is two and two, sir.

We could celebrate the revolutionary nature of this speech for many different reasons (the way it sheds and fractures the conventions of literary realism *precisely by being realistic*, for example, or the poetry of its repetitions)—but the aspect of it that I want to flag up is the way the logic of accountancy has permeated prose itself, wormed right into its bones: the passage isn't simply *about* totting up a bill; rather, the mechanism of financial computation generates what's on the page; what we read is like the paper tape that issues from an adding machine. A literal cash machine, with turning slots for shillings, sixpences, halfcrowns, and crowns appears in the next chapter, in which, while England is cast (by the schoolmaster Deasy) as a land of monetary self-sufficiency (albeit one that's threatened by usurious Jewish merchants), all of Ireland is recast (by Stephen) as a pawn-shop, one to which (we realize as he enumerates his debts) he's more in hock than most. The chapter ends in a strangely Bataillean image (more of him later), as the sun profligately flings, through a checkerwork of leaves, dancing coins on Deasy's shoulders: light itself turning into money.

Stephen's debt will re-emerge in *Scylla and Charybdis*, assert itself during his argument with the poet George "A. E." Russell (one of his many creditors) as the underlying "given" that binds his ever-changing molecules, his fraught bid for literary inheritance, and his own reserve and storehouse, the five-voweled alphabet, together: A E I O U. In Burke's pub and Bella Cohen's brothel, Stephen will be as spend-thrift as the sun, prompting Bloom to relieve him of his coins for safekeeping—which turns him, Bloom, into a cash machine as well: Bloom, son of a money-lending Jew of the type so despised by Deasy, who moves around Dublin negotiating terms and profit margins; who in his reveries hatches get-rich-quick schemes; who, ever inquisitive, marks the edge of a florin before tendering it to a grocer "for circulation on the waters of civic finance, for possible, circuitous or direct, return." In (or out of) Bloom's hands, this grubby coin turns into the eponymous Homeric hero, or the other way around: *Ulysses* becomes currency. As the milkwoman's invoice opened the Odyssean day of reckoning, so a new check will call time on it, as Joyce carries the logic of financial computation one step further still: the bill we are presented with in *Ithaca* isn't simply *like* a tabulated sum—it *is* one, reproduced unchanged in double-entry format. Bloom has fantasized repeatedly about becoming a writer, earning good cash by publishing detective stories or accounts of characters encountered at nocturnal cab shelters; this, though, is the real "account" he'll write of his day, his true act of bookkeeping.

ONE OF BLOOM'S mooted entrepreneurial schemes involves selling human waste on an industrial scale. The passage from excrement to money is one that my own Joycean
career has followed, albeit in reverse. After Trieste, Sam
Slote, a standing member of the Great Council of All Things
Joycean, invited me to the next symposium, to be held in
Dublin in 2004—Bloomsday's centenary. What would you
like to talk about? he asked. Oh, I don't know, I told him.
Joyce 'n shit. Joyce and shit? he repeated. That's good—really good. He was serious—and with reason: Joyce's work
is mired in excremental language, excremental imagery:
watercloset, commodes, sewers, "clotted hinderparts,"
"soiled goods" and "slopperish matter," "nappy spattees," "pip
poo pat" of "bulgar... bowels" and so on. There may be, as
I suggested, something eschatological about the Joyce-event,
but this comes coated in a straight-up scatology so vulgar
it would make Beavis and Butthead blush.

Nowhere is Joyce more potty-mouthed than when taking
on the language and procedure of religious devotion. At the
outset of *Finnegans Wake* the books of Genesis and Exodus
become urinary and colonic tracts and Christ the salmon
turns into a big brown trout, a "brontoichthyian" thunderfish or turd floating in a stream mingling with "piddle." Or
rather—once more—have *already* become and *already*
turned into: the counter-Midas moment, the general

en-merding, takes place (as before) in *Ulysses*. Bloom starts his day by votively bowing his head as he enters his outhouse to perform the act of defecation that will retroactively see him hailed as "Moses, Moses, King of the Jews" who "wiped his arse on the *Daily News*." Buck Mulligan, in his parody of Catholic Mass, quick-changes from priest to military doctor, peeping at an imaginary stool sample floating in what he's up to now presented as an altar-bowl and, covering it quickly up again, sends the sick man who produced it back to barracks.

The actual content of Mulligan's bowl may not be feces, but it is human waste nonetheless: unwanted stubble, cast-off skin-cells, dead matter that his body has expelled, let drop. These things, too, belong to the category of excreta, as do phlegm, bile, navel cords and blood; whatever is excessive, leaking, training, dragging or trascining. *Ulysses* is packed to overflowing with such things; or, better to say, every theme or term or concept that enters its pages, no matter how intangible or rarified, is transformed into such a thing—lowly, degraded, abject—the more so the more elevated it held itself to be before the novel's degradatory machinery took hold of it. Poetry turns into snot; nature, the very contours of the Romantic sublime, its bay and shoreline, turn into a bowl of sluggish vomit. Just as the book's economic register orchestrates a flattening of all fields, their subjection to the logic of soiled currency, so its excretative one oversees a general debasement, a downpegging of all categories to a baseline of the bodily, of bodies ingesting or discharging other bodies. Forget Apollonian beauty: what Bloom wants to know is if statues of Greek gods have assholes. For him, the heart, seat of refined emotions, is a rusty pump; communion is cannibalism; justice just "means...everybody eating everybody else." He is obsessed with falling bodies, their weight and volume and the speed at which they fall. *Ulysses* is a heavy book, a book that's full of weight: a fallen book. What has fallen in it, into it, is all that literature, and culture in general, previously held immaterial or abstract; in its pages, the ideal implodes; metaphysics collapses into (to borrow artist Jake Chapman's term) meatphysics. It's hard to think, outside of zombie movies, of a work more omnivoric—and omni-emetic. Rats eat corpses; savages eat missionaries; Bloom eats cheese; cheese eats itself; dogs eat themselves too, spew themselves out, eat themselves again; the city and the day eat and spew Bloom...

Joyce, needless to say, is a materialist. Over the neoplatonism of A. E., his trite assertion that "Art has to reveal to us ideas, formless spiritual essences," he champions Stephen's Aristotelian materialism of the now, the here, the art of forms and form. Against vague cosmic and chthonic mysticism he pits Bloom's vision of spinning gasballs—"Gas, then solid: then world: then cold: then dead shell drifting around, frozen rock"—and of "entomological organic existences concealed in cavities of the earth, beneath removable stones, in hives and mounds, of microbes, germs, bacteria, bacilli, spermatozoa." But this materialism should not be confused with empiricism. On the contrary, it's a materialism of the type that Georges Bataille, in a short text that perfectly formulates all that I've been tracking here, announces as "base materialism." For Bataille, the positivist materialism of science or the dialectical materialism of Marxism are nothing more than Christianity in disguise, and a philosophy grounded in them remains an idealist one. Against crypto-Platonic versions of "form" he proposes "the Formless," or *l'Informe*. *L'Informe*, Bataille writes in his *Critical Dictionary*,

> is not only an adjective having a given meaning, but a term that serves to bring things down . . .

[the French term he uses for "bring down" is *déclasser*, which carries the dual sense of lowering in class, or demoting, and of releasing from all classificatory or taxonomic constraints]

> . . . a term that serves to bring things down in a world that generally requires that each thing have its form. What

this word [*l'Informe*] designates has no rights in any sense and gets itself squashed everywhere, like a spider or an earthworm. In fact, for academic men to be happy, the universe would have to take shape. All of philosophy has no other goal: it is a matter of giving a frock coat to what is, a mathematical frock coat. On the other hand, affirming that the universe resembles nothing and is only *formless* [*informe*] amounts to saying that the universe is something like a spider or spit.

Bataille's vivid passage proclaims and champions what I see as one of the central thrusts of literature as it moves into and through the twentieth century—perhaps *the* central one; a thrust whose own central moment or prime axis would, for me, be *Ulysses*. You can see it swelling in late Yeats, the downgrading of his lofty esoteric icons to a clutter of half-broken rag-and-bone-shop trinkets in "The Circus Animals' Desertion"; you can see it, later, fully blown in the *proêmes* of Francis Ponge, his celebration of the endomorphic thingliness of things, the way their sheer material facticity breaches the limits of every attempt to conceptually or aesthetically contain them; or in Wallace Stevens, his plum that "survives its poems," oozing and rotting beyond and between their lines; in visual art, you can see it in the thick, muddy canvases of Dubuffet, where materiality far overtakes mimesis; or, later, in the unformed mounds of fat slapped down in front of us by Joseph Beuys. But the nucleus of this thrust; the engine room in which the process—*reverse* alchemy, let's call it—fully plays itself out, whirrs and clunks and splats and squelches through its paces; the stage on which its playing-out can be fully viewed and audited; or (let's try that term again now) its *index*, would be *Ulysses*. *Ulysses* matters most, because it makes matter of everything. Everything in *Ulysses* is *déclassé*, or (to use another term of Joyce's) "netherfallen." Things aren't even things in *Ulysses*—at least not in any quasi-autonomous sense, monadic entities in which subjective sovereignty has been re-housed, refuged or reconstituted; rather, they too are abject, broken, other things' excreta. Everything is a by-product of something else. Cheese isn't just self-consuming: it's the "corpse of milk"; jackets, soap and margarine are corpses of corpses, the offslew of hide, hair and horns disgorged by slaughterhouses—what Bloom, brilliantly, calls "the fifth quarter": not the fourth quarter but the fifth, the one that's surplus to a thing's integrity, to mathematics itself, a remainder.

By-products, or throwaways. This last word doesn't only name the horse Bloom inadvertently tips; it also designates the crumpled scrap of paper that goes drifting down the Liffey in The Wandering Rocks. Just as Joyce links literature to money, he binds it in even more solidly with base matter. Bloom's actions and preoccupations, time and again, assess the written word solely in terms of its by-products: the blotting paper that he used to sell, that he blots Martha's name with, hatching an idea for a detective story in which blotter-residues lead a sleuth to solve a crime; the giant sheet of it that he proposes the stationer Wisdom Hely parade through the streets; or the equally enormous inkbottle he also pitches Hely, "with a false stain of black celluloid" (Claes Oldenburg's entire career opens and closes in the space of that throwaway); or the actual ink, "encaustic pigment" he recalls Molly leaving her pen in, "exposed to the corrosive action of copperas, green vitriol and nutgall." His own compositional effort in Nausicaa ("I am a . . .") also gets bogged down by the material he writes on, as his stick sticks in the mud and thus becomes the very thing it tries to represent. Stephen, for his part, obsesses with the question of the word becoming flesh and flesh becoming word; he *sees* words in Eumaeus "changing color like those crabs about Ringsend in the morning burrowing quickly into all colors of different sorts of the same sand . . ."

Crabs, worms, spiders. Stephen, walking on the beach in Proteus, is walking through Bataille's *l'Informe*—affording it no rights, crushing it everywhere:

His boots trod again a damp crackling mass, razorshells, squeaking pebbles, that on the unnumbered pebbles beats, wood sieved by the shipworm, lost Armada.

He may be crushing it—but this crushing affords him no domination; on the contrary, the quagmire starts to drag him, like Bloom's stick, into its base plane:

Unwholesome sandflats waited to suck his treading soles, breathing upward sewage breath, a pocket of seaweed smouldered in seafire under a midden of man's ashes.

Slippery, treacherous, it won't sit still for him or let itself be pinned down, enumerated, mathematically frock-coated. *Déclassé* and *déclassant*, it renders impossible a certain—classical, enlightenment or romantic—model of subjective, cognitive or literary mastery. And yet it's legible, laced with the "signatures of all things I have come to read . . . coloured signs . . . language tide and wind have silted here" (or, as he also terms it, "wild sea money"). As Stephen moves through it, rhythm begins—poetic rhythm, "Acatalectic tetrameter of iambs marching." This, for me, is quite simply the primal scene of modern writing. World, whooshing, comes in waves to Stephen, in the basest form imaginable: silt, broken hoops, a boat's gunwale; fragments of other objects, their by-products or corpses—which are themselves also signs and codices, whole cultural histories (Théophile Gautier's entire oeuvre is embedded, via Louis Veuillot, in the gunwale alone) that Stephen, practicing a kind of haptic semiotics, crushcrackcricks his way through, "scann[ing]" the shore as his feet sink into its sockets. Which, in turn, makes writing stir—not in the tranquil, Wordsworthian guise of a *fait accompli*, but restlessly, as no more than potentiality and fragment. Stephen's first line is itself a by-product, a corpse-part of the decomposing verse he's replayed moments earlier:

> Won't you come to Sandymount,
> Madeline the mare?

degrades itself, agallop, into

> deline the mare

—a line, or half-line, that itself suggests the very act that Stephen's doing, his delineating of the sea, or rather his delineating of space itself, his erasure and re-inscription of its lines and borders. Writing on Bataille, the art critic Yves-Alain Bois proffers the term "pulsation," which involves an endless beat that punctures the disembodied self-closure of pure visuality and incites an irruption of the carnal . . . Once the unified visual field is agitated by a shake-up that irremediably punctures the screen of its formality and populates it with organs, there is "pulsation."

He could be describing Stephen's beach—a place in which the visual field has been punctured by an irruption of the carnal. It is spattered with organs, a diaphane in bodies: bladderwrack, sockets, swaying arms, a redpanting tongue, a bloated carcass, "bag of corpsegas sopping in foul brine." Zombie omnivorism names the very possibility of literature, as "Dead breaths I living breathe, tread dead dust, devour a urinous offal from all dead." Cut to Bloom, who devours a urinous offal from all dead before going off to watch "HOW," as Joyce announces in capital letters, "A GREAT DAILY ORGAN IS TURNED OUT."

The organ Bloom watches being turned out is, of course, a newspaper; what is being dismembered, cut up in proto-Burroughsian (the adding machine's scion) fashion is—again—snatches of prose. Language, in *Ulysses*, is just another organ—and, like so many other organs in this genuinely obscene book, it keeps getting unzipped, whipped out, flashed left and right and center. Critics and teachers should desist, once and for all, from using the term "interior mono-logue" to describe the novel's trademark outbreaks of unas-signed first-person narrative. This is not interior monologue; it's exterior consciousness, embodied—or encorpsed—con-sciousness that has ruptured conventional syntax's membrane, prolapsed. Turned out, fallen, consciousness and language lie and drift around Dublin's streets like ozone in dystopian sci-fi fables: H and E and L, printed on sandwich-boards, march along the gutter while Y lags behind, cramming a chunk of bread into his mouth. Even the novel's letters eat and crap! Michel Leiris, Bataille's co-author of the *Dictio-nary*, describes, in *Scratches*, eating alphabetti spaghetti as a child; eating too much, and consequently being sick; watch-ing the dented letters fall back from him: far from being a tool for refining the world into concepts, language is what mixes with saliva in your mouth, gets kneaded by your tongue and teeth, repeats on you. Joyce knows this all too well:

> Yum. Softly she gave me in my mouth the seedcake warm and chewed. Mawkish pulp her mouth had mumbled sweetsour of her spittle. Joy: I ate it: joy. Young life, her lips that gave me pouting. Soft warm sticky gumjelly lips.

This scene, repeated not just once but twice (Molly re-plays it too), itself reprises Stephen's half-formed (or half-deformed) vampire-poem (written on a torn-off scrap of Deasy's foot-and-mouth letter) in which *mouth to her mouth's kiss* degrades into *mouth to her moomb*, then *oomb, allwombing tomb*, then finally *mouth to my mouth*. But it's the seedcake episode, and not the slight, if suggestive, poem, that for me most amplifies and makes resonate, re-sound, the field of potentiality, literary potentiality, that has lain immanent, or imminent, throughout the novel. Seedcake, not fruitcake or carrot cake: this is a scene of both fertility and (to use one of Derrida's favorite terms) dissemination; writing as material transmission, repetition, pulp of joyful, sweetsour mumbling.

AND YET neither the seed-spitting nor the vampire poem are, at this point, in and of themselves, the work, any more than Bloom's tabulated bill is. The work, at this point, remains to be written. To put it another way: *Ulysses* is (like several of Thomas Bernhard's novels) a book in which the central stake is the coming-into-being of the book itself. This, effectively, is what Stephen is tasked with: to write *Ulysses*. "I want you to write something," says Miles Crawford. "You can do it. Put us all into it, damn its soul." He has in mind a piece of long-form journalism, but the exhortation, for both Stephen and the reader, carries far, far wider implications, especially when the press-headline repeats it (in block capitals once more): "YOU CAN DO IT!" "All desire to see you bring forth the work you meditate," Lenehan tells Stephen in Oxen of the Sun, after the latter has encircled his own head with a putative laurel, drunkenly boasting of his bard's ability to make "ghosts troop to my call." Actually, it's the ghosts who order him, and Stephen knows it; knows of the coffined, mummified, word-embalmed thoughts in Dublin's library that "an itch of death is in them, to tell me in my ear a maudlin tale, urge me to wreak their will." Here another sense of Bataille's term *déclasser* suggests itself, a decidedly twenty-first-century one: declassification: Stephen as a kind of hacker, called upon to dicky into sealed and buried files, to crack them open, break their contents out again, so that these may commingle, necroactively cross-pollinate to produce new effects, new situations. For the political theorist McKenzie Wark, to hack is simply "to produce the plane upon which different things may enter into relation"—which, in turn, breaches open a fresh field of space-time, the grounds of possibility for the new creative event. Stephen, like his predecessor Hamlet, has been ghost- (or corpse-) called; where Hamlet's orders were to act (orders that he disobeys by instead writing), Stephen's orders, from the outset, are to write. Nonetheless, he's as useless at carrying them out as Hamlet. Stephen, I'd suggest—and it's impossible, when pointing at Stephen, not to also finger Joyce himself—is as agonized as Anthony Burgess, agonized to the point of paralysis, by the same question: How do you write after *Ulysses*—*if* we take *Ulysses* to mean the plane of possibility breached or hacked open by the extraordinary creative wave on whose breaking crest he finds himself borne—or, perhaps, to downgrade the surfing metaphor, within whose surging foam he finds himself submerged. No wonder he's both afraid of and fascinated by the sea.

The main ghost in the library may be Hamlet's—although Hamlet is already, as Deleuze and Guattari would put it, quite a crowd: Hamlet Senior, Hamlet Junior, Shakespeare, Hamnet, Bloom, Rudis Senior and Junior, Stephen's mother, and so forth. But the ghost that interests me most here—one that glides just fleetingly through the chief librarian's office—is that of another Stephen: Mallarmé, who in his own essays depicts Hamlet "reading the book of himself" and "struggling beneath the curse of having to *appear*." If Joyce has a rival as a framer of modernity in terms of tombs and crypts and corpses, it's the Mallarmé of *Igitur*; if he has a rival as purveyor of *the* rapturous event of literary modernity, it's the Mallarmé of *Un Coup de Des*. Like *Ulysses, Un*

Coup enacts the ruin of a certain type of cultural space, a certain model of subjective and creative mastery, enacts the wave-tossed breakdown, degradation, atomization of ship into gunwale, language into typographic fragments—a shattering and breaking that, in their very destructiveness, prize open the abyssal space in which the decisive new poetic act might "happen" or emerge: like *Ulysses*, it grasps after "a movement . . . an actuality of the possible as possible."

Not only, as critics have already noticed, is *Un Coup*, its imagery, scenarios, even vocabulary, hacked up and re-devoured, regurgitated in the text of *Ulysses* (once you've started noticing it—the shipwrecked sailors, mermaids, obsessions with numbers and computations and so on—it's everywhere: Stephen on the beach could even be said to be reenacting *Un Coup*, pacing out poetry as spacing, *nach* and *neben*, marking signs on a white field); but Joyce's novel, just like Mallarmé's poem, is dominated by its own anticipatory or "futural" relation to the looming specter of a work-to-come. Mallarmé famously claims in *Le Livre—Instrument Spirituel* that "everything in the world exists in order to end up in a book." The conventional "book" being insufficient to the task of storing and transforming the whole world, Mallarmé starts deforming the book, cracking its ribs and spine, folding out its pages in a bid to overhaul it into the expanded *livre* that *would* be up to the job: these are the terms and context under which *Un Coup* is written. But, as Maurice Blanchot points out, we should not, nor did Mallarmé, see *Un Coup as* this *über-livre*'s realization; rather "it is its reserve and its forever hidden presence, the risk of its venture, the measure of its limitless challenge."

Reserve, risk, venture: here the economic field asserts itself once more. Shakespeare's Timon of Athens, manically apostrophizing the gold he's dug up from the ground, simultaneously curses it as a "defiler" *and* marvels at the way it "solder'st close impossibilities/and makest them kiss"—the latter capacity, of course, being precisely the one McKenzie Wark attributes to the hack. Joyce seems to intuit the same connection: *Ulysses*'s economic register, grubby though it is, also underwrites a giant speculative system in which, amidst collapse and boom, the promise of a monumental or unprecedented return gestates; the promise of literature *as* this return; a promise that remains deferred—indeed, whose deferral is necessary for the speculative system's very existence. Where the critic William Carpenter sees *Ulysses* "as" the Mallarméan Book, I'd want to keep it in the same frame but view it from the flipside, as the exact inverse—doubly so. Mallarmé's Book cannot be written, but the demand to do so, once it has been issued, sets the parameters of future serious literature. *Ulysses* inhabits these impossible parameters, these parameters of impossibility—and consequently is not only *not* the Book heralded by Mallarmé, but also not the book anticipated or announced *by itself.* When you read it, you're reading what's actually *there* always in relation to a framework that's not "there," mundane contemporary events always in terms of an epic ur-historical "outside" that remains outside, its reflection appearing inside only by inversion. Bloom is not Odysseus, nor Molly Penelope; every Homeric link is effected as a negative, a gap, the distance between (for example) a Cyclops-blinding poker and chimney-sweep's brush, or a siren's foam-lashed rock and a beer-flecked bar counter, or an Aeolian harp-string and a strip of dental floss; there is no heroic or redemptive reconciliation between Bloom and Molly; no resurrection of the dead; even Molly's landmark speech remains unspoken. Just as history, for Stephen, is a repository or storeroom of all the events that failed to happen, infinite ousted possibilities, so the whole "story" of *Ulysses* takes place in the negative, a place where, ultimately (to quote Mallarmé), nothing will have taken place except the place. The movement toward almost miraculous actuality, impossible to possible, is at every instant set in motion *and* held in abeyance, in reserve, displaced or "offset" from a reality that might be consummated *as* reality onto the disjecta-symbols of another, un-realized totality: onto potted meats, keys and Keyes ads, the trajectories of urine, menstrual blood in a chamber pot.

Form, the formless, speculation: that's what it comes down to. This last term, "speculation," in addition to its economic and intellectual connotations, carries an astronomic meaning: contemplation of the heavens. And it's within the umbra of this meaning that the largest of *Un Coup*'s shadows hides itself in *Ulysses*. Like Mallarmé's poem, Joyce's novel is full of constellational imagery. Stephen repeatedly invokes the delta of Cassiopeia—"the recumbent constellation," as he notes in Scylla and Charybdis, that hung over Shakespeare's birth. In The Wandering Rocks he pictures stars flung by archangels to the wormy earth, to be rooted out by pigs and poets. The link between poetic words, their formatting and spacing, and the layout of the stars is crucial to the climax of *Un Coup*, whose high point (literally) is the Septentrion or North Star—a point at which a "place" would fuse with its own beyond, and for that very reason a point never attained, but in whose orbit thought, writing-as-thought, rolls and flashes sidereally across the gutter of the page, numbering its *compte total en formation*, forming its inky account. The same climactic movement builds up at the end of *Ulysses*, which sweeps us from the North Star Hotel on to a barrage of meditations on constellations: the milky way, Arcturus, equinoxes, nascent new stars and "the parallax or parallactic drift of socalled fixed stars, in reality evermoving wanderers." After these meditations, Bloom, as we know, tots up his own account, then pictures himself navigating, "septentrional, by night the polestar," wandering "to the extreme limit of his cometary orbit ... to the extreme boundary of space, passing from land to land, among peoples, amid events." But this, of course, is all speculation; what he actually *does* is lie in bed, viewing his lodestar Molly from the wrong end.

Parallax, we should note in passing, hits on the one counter-intuitive meaning of a term that kicked this whole discussion off: the "absolute magnitude" of a star is "the apparent magnitude which the star would have if it was transferred to a distance from the sun corresponding to a parallax of 0"1." In constellational terms, absolute is as relative as index. If Bloom is always elsewhere, beyond himself, this is because *Ulysses* is always elsewhere and beyond itself as well; lost absolutely in its index, it moves in the orbit of its own beyond; just as it carries its own wake in it, it carries its own elsewhere in it too, or rather lets this elsewhere carry it, training, dragging and trascining it, load and lode. Which means that it carries the *novel* in it, as elsewhere: book-to-come, a possibility in impossible form.

How to write *after Ulysses*? What would this question even mean? Time, in *Ulysses*, is fallen too, a by-product of earth-pulled bodies; Dunsink done sunk, and the hours dance across a brothel floor. Joyce-time no longer moves in a straight line from past to future; rather, it, too, accretes and self-consumes: future plunges back into past, "now" being the transit-point or orifice through which this involution passes. When Stephen tells us as much in the library he's sketching out a new type of *cultural* time that we could say Joyce's work inaugurates: a time not of cultural progress, even from one vanguard to the next, but rather one in which culture will also involute, consume its own tail, its actors becoming agents as and when they join the never-ending zombie eucharist.

By the *Wake*, this involuted schema will be fixed as a Viconian one of *ricorso* or reenactment, in which objects and situations, far from being apotheosized or sublimated, bob about and return (albeit in slightly different form). This schema is already evident in *Ulysses*, its recirculation of detritus in the form of things, images, events, its many instances of "history repeating itself," as Bloom puts it, "with a difference." But the temporal metronome to whose beat *Ulysses*'s hours most dance is (I'd suggest), once more that of constellation—understood now in its Benjaminian sense, as a cross- or trans-historical (and necessarily arbitrary or relative) joining-up of disparate or previously unconnected points—a joining-up that generates a sudden flash of paradoxical simultaneity, the revolutionary ground for a whole new realm of understanding. If you like, another hack. This is the hack performed by Molly, as, lying on a plane on the 53rd parallel of latitude north, and the 6th meridian of longitude west, she places the City Arms Hotel, Ontario Terrace and Howth Head and a soup-altercation waiting for a train and an ankle-spraining incident at a party and the Greeks and the Jews and the Arabs and the sea and Bloom and Stephen all on a plane of constellated simultaneity. It's a constellation that can only be construed from elsewhere, parallactically. Even as she plots her ties to Stephen, he has already wandered off; the very stars presiding over her are fading, and their light is years old anyhow; beside which, the revolving earth is sending them, like Gabriel Conroy, Westwards. But an alignment has taken place; a conjunction been passed through; an event-plane hewn into appearance: the event-plane of the word itself, its own unfolding elsewhere. That's why *Ulysses* matters. Where Stephen, like Cordelia, says Nothing (or, after Siegfried, Nothung), Molly carries negative logic to its outer limit by not saying anything at all—but then I don't need to tell you what the very last word that she doesn't say is.

2013

Kool Thing, or Why I Want to Fuck Patty Hearst

I REMEMBER, in 1992 or so, listening to Kim Gordon's voice monologuing over the Sonic Youth song "Kool Thing." She was talking about a white girl lying on a bed with a dagger in her hand, staring at a black panther in a tree; and she said it had something to do with Patty Hearst. I didn't know who Patty Hearst was then. Years later, when I visited the Joyce Museum in the gun-tower where he spent the night that Ulysses *emerged from, there was a life-sized black panther in the bedroom: Joyce's roommate, like his hero Stephen's, had a nightmare with one in it and, picking a gun up in his half sleep from the night table beside his bed, fired it over Joyce's head. Beneath the bedroom was a storeroom for gunpowder; in past centuries the guardians of the tower had to be careful not to generate any sparks. Maybe all avant-gardes begin with gunpowder and a dream of a black panther.*

I IMAGINE HER standing in a bathrobe and alpaca slippers, her hair still wet from the shower, her fingers sticky from the homemade pastry she's been rolling on her kitchen counter. I imagine peering at her through the front door's frosted glass, her face distending as she moves behind it; or how it looks from her side, the figures dark and imprecise against the night, the stick-shapes by their waists she doesn't know are guns. Or later, after they've knocked her down and carted her off to their hideout, the way she squints through a black eye at the TV screen, watching the news, seeing the building where she lived all cordoned off by police-tape, reporters crowded round her mother who wears black, and thinking: *No, that's wrong, it's she who's dead, not me. My father standing beside her is dead as well. And the detectives, anchormen and commentators, the others too, everyone behind the screen: all distant, unreal, dead.*

I picture her sitting in the closet with its musty carpet and rubber-foam mattress, its soundproofing pads that smell of old sweat, listening to the radio they've placed there with her, listening hour after hour, like Orphée, as the song-lyrics, bulletins and station-idents run together, all the voices blurring: disc jockeys, announcers, lonely nighttime callers. I hear her solitude in theirs, and theirs in hers, and in both of these the solitude of fur-trappers and gold-prospectors, bums and traveling salesmen, taxi drivers and night watchmen, a continental loneliness booming and echoing through centuries. And behind all these, I hear the solitude of her own grandfather: the only child, estranged husband, jealous sugar-daddy, would-be president who couldn't get the people to like him enough to elect him so had his own world built for him to rule over and peopled it with elephants and zebras, lions, tigers, tahr goats, monkeys; filled its dining halls and billiard rooms with gargoyles, frescoes, tapestries and kantharoi; obliged his guests to watch each evening the films, still unreleased, that he'd produced; forced them to wear fancy-dress so they would all stay behind masks; forbade them to speak of death, which made the word hang in the air unspoken all the time; stayed up long after they and all the butlers, gardeners, gamekeepers and switchboard operators had gone to sleep and, reclining on his four-poster beneath a painting of Napoleon alone before the Sphinx, would drift off to the sound of panthers shrieking in the night.

I imagine her hairs bristling as she tells her parents that they're bourgeois pigs and that she'll never come back home; her voice crackling with excitement as she reads onto a tape the revolutionary statement that will soon be played on every radio and television station in the country. I see her eyes blaze like coal fires as she poses with a machine gun in front of the Egyptian symbol painted on the wall: the seven-headed cobra Wadjet, Lady of Devouring Flame, Wadjet the Invincible whose presence causes malachite to glisten, she who lives according to her will, the pupil in the eye of Re the sun, who hisses: *Few approach me. The confederacy of Seth is at my side and what is near me burns.*

I picture her as the heroine of the pulp-porn novel published several years before her kidnapping in which a black man steals a debutante named Patricia, locks her in a hideaway and has his way with her until the negro semen pickling her brain makes her a criminal. I wonder if her kidnappers had read it, then realize that it doesn't matter: it's all fiction, the whole thing. I tell myself she understands this, and that she's letting the story play itself out by assuming the main role.

I picture her as Tania, Che's lover; as Ophelia the teenage suicide; as Antigone the goth; as Sylvia Plath, panther-stalked girl who never had a gun placed in her hands but stuck her head inside an oven; as Molly Bloom who lies in bed bleeding, thinking of all the men she's had; as Stephen Dedalus, boy-Cordelia who hears the ruin of all space, shattered glass and toppling masonry, and time one livid final flame; as James Joyce himself, who summoned it all up from a dream of a black panther; or as his favorite child Lucia, the mad spark who cracked under the weight of her inheritance. I picture her as the Statue of Liberty holding a stick of dynamite instead of a torch. I picture her as Lara Croft, Raider of Tombs, running through urban landscapes out of Eldridge Cleaver: armored vehicles crisscrossing city streets, black smoke billowing against the daylight sky, the sound of Tommy-guns and snipers' rifles, barbed wire closing off whole sections of the city, "and everywhere the smell of cordite."

I see her riding in a car through San Francisco with the window wound down, breeze tickling her hair and flapping her donkey jacket's collar, the untinned air and clear blue daylight making her giddy; then running from the car into a bank, shouting her name out as she waves her gun at terrified customers and staff. I picture the movements of the other revolutionaries as they vault the counters, throw open the cash drawers; the cascade of glass as the bullet-peppered windows crystallize and fall; the screech of the car's tires as it pulls off again; and her, staring back through the rear window as the bank and street and people drain away and the world retreats again behind a screen.

Like Orphée through the silver mirror: Patty in the Zone. I see her multiplying into a thousand different women as the hotlines set up in her name jam up with calls reporting sightings of her in supermarkets, cinemas and cafes, pool halls, libraries and trains. She's morphing from a typist in Louisiana to a hitchhiker in Tennessee, a croupier in Vegas, Sacramento dancer, toll collector on the Arizona interstate, a hundred New York students, seven hundred California teenagers—and splitting further in kaleidoscopes of fantasies and dreams, her image broken down to arsenals of double-gauges, thirty-calibers and twelve-bores, grenades and pipe bombs, angles of limbs on shadows of assassins climbing staircases at night. And she becomes some of these images, some of the characters as well: dressing as an airline stewardess, a hotel clerk, a secretary—or, when she and her comrades leave San Francisco for Los Angeles, a jazz musician, face blacked up and instrument case full of weapons. I see her looking at the traffic on the freeway, playing with the radio, always the radio, hearing revolutionary subtexts in the songs and sympathetic propaganda in the interference between broadcast areas; then, cruising round Watts and Compton, seeing the ruined houses and the gutted busses, thinking: *Yes, this is the Zone, and it's begun, the final uprising, the crisis, the dénouement.*

I understand she has to miss it, like a lead player wandering offstage in some anxious dream and getting waylaid among props and curtain ropes. There's a *correctness* in her decision to go shopping for provisions just before the police swoop on the house with armored cars; and in the way she hears it, on the radio (where else?); and the way she checks into a Disneyland motel and turns the TV on to see the house go up in flames, one of her friends run out and have her lungs ripped from her chest by bullets, blood shoot back-wards from another's head, the rest burning inside, the angle changing slightly with each channel. I picture her biting her hand to stifle screams, the makeup running down her face, her body bouncing on the bed, and think: this is the Patty Hearst I want to fuck—not the chat-show guest or irony-trophy movie extra she became, but this one here. I want to fuck this one because this one's America: all of it, sitting in a motel bedroom, watching the apocalypse on television.

2008

Get Real, or What Jellyfish Have to Tell Us About Literature

I.

IN THE INTRODUCTION to his 1973 masterpiece *Crash*, J. G. Ballard ponders what he calls "the balance between fiction and reality." "We live," he writes,

> in a world ruled by fictions of every kind—mass-merchandizing, advertising, politics conducted as a branch of advertising, the pre-empting of any original response to experience by the television screen. We live inside an enormous novel. It is now less and less necessary for the writer to invent the fictional content of his novel. The fiction is already there. The writer's task is to invent the reality.

The paragraphs that follow are a little disappointing, as Ballard unquestioningly endorses, firstly, a psychologism (the writer "offers the reader the contents of his own head"), then a positivism (he must "devise hypotheses and test them against the facts"), then a moralism (the main purpose of his novel is a cautionary one, a warning against a brutal technological future)—all of which *isms* now seem both dated and misplaced. But there's still something here we can hold onto; something vital. And it hinges on this word *invent*. Ballard doesn't tell us that a novelist should "discover" or "intuit" or "reveal" reality: they must *invent* it. Reality's not there yet; it is something to be brought forth or produced; and this producing is the charge, duty and stake of writing.

There's been a lot of talk in recent years about reality in fiction; or reality *versus* fiction; a hunger for the real; a realism which is realistic set against an avant-garde which isn't; and so on. I find this talk enticing and frustrating in equal measure. Actually, not in equal measure: I find it more frustrating than enticing. That half a century after Foucault's relentless charting of the constructedness of all social contexts and knowledge categories; or, indeed, a century and a half after Nietzsche's lyrical unmasking of truth itself as no more than "a mobile army of metaphors, metonymics, anthropomorphisms . . . a sum of human relations . . . poetically and rhetorically intensified . . . illusions of which one has forgotten that they *are* illusions"; not to mention other landmark interventions we might think of (those of Marx,

Derrida, Lyotard, Kristeva, Deleuze-Guattari, and so forth)
—that after all these, such simplistic oppositions can be
proffered in the name of critical reflection on the novel is
disheartening. It seems to me completely meaningless, or at
least unproductive, to discuss such things unless, to borrow
a formulation from the "realist" writer Raymond Carver,
we first ask what we talk about when we talk about the real.
And the first move in this direction would be to unpick the
very terms *the real, reality,* and *realism.*

II.

Let's start with *realism,* since it's the easiest target of the
lot—a sitting duck, in fact. What is it? It's a literary convention—no more, no less. As such, it's as laden with artifice as
any other literary convention. Ford Madox Ford, in a passage
from *Joseph Conrad: A Personal Remembrance,* brilliantly
skewers the implicit claim a certain prose style—that of realism—makes to faithfully and objectively reflect, capture
or report on historical events and mental activity:

> Life does not say to you: In 1914 my next-door neighbour,
> Mr. Slack, erected a greenhouse and painted it with Cox's
> green aluminium paint.... If you think about the matter
> you will remember, in various unordered pictures, how

one day Mr. Slack appeared in his garden and contemplated the wall of his house. You will then try to remember the year of that occurrence and you will fix it as August 1914 because having had the foresight to bear the municipal stock of the City of Liège you were able to afford a first-class season ticket for the first time in your life. You will remember Mr. Slack—then much thinner because it was before he found out where to buy that cheap Burgundy of which he has since drunk an inordinate quantity though whisky you think would be much better for him! Mr. Slack again came into his garden, this time with a pale, weaselly-faced fellow, who touched his cap from time to time. Mr. Slack will point to his house-wall several times at different points, the weaselly fellow touching his cap at each pointing. Some days after, coming back from business you will have observed against Mr. Slack's wall.... At this point you will remember that you were then the manager of the fresh-fish branch of Messrs. Catlin and Clovis in Fenchurch Street.... What a change since then! Millicent had not yet put her hair up.... You will remember how Millicent's hair looked, rather pale and burnished in plaits. You will remember how it now looks, henna'd: and you will see in one corner of your mind's eye a little picture of Mr. Mills the vicar talking—oh, very kindly— to Millicent after she has come back from Brighton....

But perhaps you had better not risk that. You remember some of the things said by means of which Millicent has made you cringe—and her expression!...Cox's Aluminium Paint!...You remember the half empty tin that Mr. Slack showed you—he had a most undignified cold—with the name in a horseshoe over a blue circle that contained a red lion asleep in front of a real-gold sun....

Once we've stopped snickering at the conjunction of the words *Slack*, *erect* and *Cox* (which, given the coy erotics of the passage, the way Millicent moves and stirs beneath its link-ups, strikes me as far from accidental), we have little choice, whatever our aesthetic disposition, but to surrender to Ford's argument. This is, of course, exactly how both events and memory of them proceed: associatively, digressing, sliding, jolting, looping. William Burroughs makes the same point when discussing his cut-up technique:

Take a walk down a city street....You have seen a person cut in two by a car, bits and pieces of street signs and advertisements, reflections from shop windows—a montage of fragments...Consciousness *is* a cut-up; life is a cut-up.

He's right as well: we don't walk down the street saying to ourselves "As I walk down the street, comma, I contemplate the question of faith, or adultery, or x or y or z." A paradox emerges: that the twentieth-century avant-garde often paints a far more *realistic* picture of experience than nineteenth-century realists ever did. A second paradox, though, is that realism's founders (if not their descendants) fully appreciate the scaffolding of artifice holding their carefully-wrought edifices up, and take delight, from time to time, in shoving poles and ladders through the parlor windows. Flaubert may have written *Madame Bovary*, but he also wrote *Bouvard and Pécuchet*, in which two semi-educated men try to translate a series of cultural paradigms ("being" a gentleman gardener, "being" an aesthete or a lover) into experiences that they might live (or re-live) in an "authentic" manner, even reenacting the postures from book illustrations in their bid for this imagined authenticity—with effects as farcical as those produced by their own sixteenth-century predecessor Don Quixote. Balzac may have generated all the counts and countesses of his *comédie humaine*—rounded characters that have prompted countless readers to express their admiration for the way they seem to live and breathe as though imbued with life—but his novella *Sarrasine* is a ruthless laying bare of the very mechanism through which this fantasy (that of the "natural" and complete) operates. In mistaking a castrato—an inherently *in*complete being, a simulacrum that has no original—for the most genuine and unadulterated embodiment of woman, whom he then adopts as the source and origin of his own art, the sculptor Sarrasine enacts the system-error at the source of realism itself. When his error is revealed (in a move that imbues not life but death), both he and Balzac's readers are confronted with the fact that (as Roland Barthes puts it in his seminal 1970 reading of Balzac's piece) "realism (badly named, at any rate often badly interpreted) consists not in copying the real but in copying a (depicted) copy of the real … through secondary mimesis, [it] copies what is already a copy." It is surely no coincidence that Bouvard and Pécuchet are, like Melville's Bartleby, trained as copy-clerks.

The biggest paradox here is that the nineteenth-century realists seem to have taken a counter-realist impulse much further than the twentieth-century anti-realists. While both Ford and Burroughs post some kind of fundamental claim to depict lived life accurately, to have helped pioneer new and radical ways of doing so, Balzac and Flaubert whip the rug out from under the very possibility of doing this in any way at all, radical or not. What opens up beneath the place where this co-weft-and-warp of life and art once stood, the place we wrongly thought a solid floor was, is an abyss, endlessly regressive, of code on code, convention on convention, reading of reading of reading. (It's telling that Flaubert's last text, the endpoint to which this trajectory carries him, his final template for both literature and life, is nothing other than a dictionary: the *Dictionary of Received Ideas* into which *Bouvard and Pécuchet* tapers off.) That such blatant and splendid takedowns of naturalism, such eviscerations of any notion that writing might operate as a faithful, penetrative rendering of a reality itself unmediated, are written right into the source code of the realist tradition makes the naive or uncritical realism dominating contemporary middlebrow fiction, and the doctrine of authenticity peddled on creative writing classes the world over, all the more simple-minded.

III.

So much for realism. What, though, of the real? In a short scene from Nabokov's novel *Ada* (a multilayered tale of brother-sister incest), the young hero Van visits the shop of Mrs. Tapirov, yet another copyist: people bring her *objets d'art* and antique furniture and she makes faithful reproductions of them. As I wrote this essay I couldn't remember what it was that Van has brought for Mrs. Tapirov to copy; digging out my copy of the novel, I realized that Van doesn't remember either, that Nabokov has deliberately elided or left blank the spot, actual or conceptual, in which original should stand. As Van waits to collect his goods, he idly strokes the flowers sitting in a vase on the counter—imitation ones, of course, like everything else in the shop—and suddenly finds himself

cheated of the sterile texture his fingertips had expected when cool life kissed them with pouting lips. "My daughter," said Mrs. Tapirov, who saw his surprise, "always puts a bunch of real ones among the fake *pour attraper le client.* You drew the joker."

An extraordinary scene, intensely (or, once more, regressively) allegorical. The term *mimesis* has an ancient connection to a type of flower (the mimosa's contortions when touched were said in Aristotle's time to mimic the grimaces of mime); Mrs. Tapirov's artificial bloom-bunches not only imitate real ones but also stand for imitation itself, for all artifice, not least that of fiction-making. And there's a *real* one hid among them: a real one pretending to be a fake one pretending to be a real one. Within this playing deck constantly being shuffled and re-dealt, a joker lurks that, like a shark, might break surface and leap out at you, jaws snapping, at any time: the real. What *is* this real, though? In a novel as full of Russian childhoods as *Ada* is, albeit ones grafted onto East-Coast America, cross-pollinated by a mish-mash of linguistic transpositions, genetically modified by encrypted literary histories and watered with variants on Nabokov's own name, it's tempting to ascribe to this real the contours of some personal family secret; to ascribe by extension to the novel, and perhaps to Nabokov's whole oeuvre, the status of Mrs. Tapirov's shop: an emporium of simulations and reflections in which this real might be paraded right before *le client*, remaining hidden by being disguised as the copy of what it actually is.

Alternatively, we could go less literal and instead think sideways or inversely, discerning another set of contours: ones whose coordinates are outlined in negative, by *not* being drawn. Perec's *La Disparition* famously contains no letter *e*—not only the letter most used in French (as English) prose, but also the core of the words *père* and *mère*. Both of Perec's parents having fallen victim to the Nazis (father in battle, mother in Auschwitz), several critics have astutely heard in the French *e* its homophone *eux*, them. The real that lurks beneath the playfulness and play thus becomes, in this instance, both a personal and a historical one, the joker card a marker for the twentieth century's least funny moment. The same real—in particular the holocaust—could be attributed to all of Beckett's work, whose unnameables and catastrophes and air full of cries convey the horror and unspeakability of this event to which they never refer far more profoundly than the directly representational writing of, say, Primo Levi. The claim of an exterior historical facticity to embody a work's unspoken real is most lucidly stated, iron-ically enough, by one of Nazism's intellectual architects, Carl Schmitt, who, writing on *Hamlet*, sees in the murder of James I's father a lodestar or true north that, although absent in the text itself, orients all its compasses, making England—or, rather, Scotland—the real of Denmark, and the real of medieval Danish politics the modern Elizabethan court.

This line of thinking is both appealing and risky: appeal-ing because it frames the fictional text as a cryptic and neg-ative space haunted (like Elsinore) by the ghost of what it has excluded; risky because it sails close to the rocks of bi-ographical or historical reductionism: find the real, "solve" the work. It's not the fact that James I's father was murdered that makes *Hamlet* monumental, nor some putative inces-tuous episode in Nabokov's past that renders *Ada* rich and captivating. While I don't want to lose sight of this version entirely, I'd like to think of the real in more *structural* terms. Michel Leiris, in his essay "Literature Considered as a Bull-fight," compares the writer to a toreador. Imagine a bullfight without the bull: it would comprise a set of aesthetic ma-neuvers, pretty twirls and pirouettes and so forth—but there'd be no danger. The bull, crucially, brings this to the party; and for Leiris, *that's* the real: the tip of the bull's horn. He, too, goes on to disappoint, by proffering candid expo-sures of intimate personal peccadilloes as instances of dalliance with bullhorns—a confessional logic that would elevate Oprah's sofa to the high throne from which all writing was assessed and legitimated. But, once more, there's something to hold onto here. Leiris's conceit is rich in ways that even he seems not to realize. Think about it: if a matador is gored, the bullfight, its entire spectacle, suddenly shudders to an appalled halt; what the bull's horn brings to the party is not just danger but also the very thing that would catastrophically interrupt the party, plunging craft into chaos. If the bullfight is an analogue for literature, and if the bull's horn gives us a vision of the real (and I concur with Leiris on both these propositions), then it's a vision of the real not as a fact or secret, nor as a correspondence between the writer's work and the empirically-understood world, but rather an *event* that would involve the violent rupture of the very form and procedure of the work itself. This rupture—*nota bene*—is emphatically *not* the same thing as authenticity.

Given that I started this whole essay with Ballard, I'd suggest that *Crash* enacts, in its finale, something close to this sudden intercession of the catastrophic real. The novel's hero Vaughan, compulsive simulator of other people's car crashes (Jayne Mansfield's, Albert Camus's, James Dean's etc.), which he repeatedly re-stages with consummate skill and stylization (which makes him as much a proxy for the figure of artist or writer as Leiris's matador), plots a "perfect" car crash in which his own vehicle will collide with Elizabeth Taylor's (not a stand-in this time, but the actual actress—that is, the genuine stand-in) at the precise moment of his orgasm: a supremely-wrought marriage of *techné*, spectacle, sex, death and all the rest. He finds out when her car will pass such-and-such a spot, and plots the angles and trajectories and speed at which his own must meet it—but, disastrously, gets it fractionally wrong, misses her by inches and drowns in his own blood. Thus Vaughan, who has been in thousands of car crashes, meets with his first—and final—*accident*. The matador is gored; the shark breaks surface and wreaks havoc; a real of the type that I suggest we should embrace and celebrate punctures the screen or strip of film, destroying it: a real that *happens*, or forever threatens to do so, not as a result of the artist "getting it right" or overcoming inauthenticity, but rather as a radical and disastrous eruption *within* the always-and-irremediably inauthentic; a traumatic real; a real that's linked to repetition; a real whose framework of comprehension is ultimately neither literary nor philosophical but psychoanalytic: the real that Lacan defines as "that which always returns to the same place" *and* as "that which is unassimilable by any system of representation." The challenge, for the writer, would never be one of depicting this real realistically, or even "well"; but of approaching it in the full knowledge that, like some roving black hole, it represents (although that's not the right word anymore) the point at which the writing's entire project crumples and implodes.

IV.

The same question persists though: what would this real *be*? What form might it take? Leiris's own writing might point us toward one possible answer: matter. In the "Critical Dictionary"—note Flaubert's final literary model resurfacing—Leiris and his co-author Georges Bataille (whose own short novel *Story of the Eye* contains the most stunning matador-goring episode in all of literature—forget Hemingway), imagine a dictionary that would "begin when it no longer gives the meaning of words, but their tasks." One of the more notable of these "tasks" (I've recently tried to unpack this in relation to Joyce's writing) comes under the heading "Formless," which envisages existence as a relentless and on-going process of *deformation* that releases objects, and the world, the entire universe, from all categories and classes of the knowable and denotable until it "resembles nothing"; and envisages a philosophy and aesthetics, or counter-aesthetics, that would affirm this formlessness. Viewed from this position, a thing's real would be touched in its own materiality: a sticky, messy and above all *base* materiality that overflows all boundaries damming in the thing's—and everything's—identity, and thus threatens ontology itself. "Matter," Bataille writes elsewhere, "can only be defined as that non-logical difference that represents in relation to the economy of the universe what crime represents in relation to the law."

Van's flowers, by this measure, wouldn't be a portal through which the real enters; rather, their smelly, pouting, wet-lipped, finger-smudging physicality would themselves *constitute* the real; facticity would reside *in* them, or explode out of them, splattering Van with a real-ness that neither Mrs. Tapirov's craft-emporium nor the entire architecture of *Ada* could manage or contain. Bataille's real is the material real that Francis Ponge spent his entire creative life failing to manage, the failure itself forming the *raison d'être* of his work. What happens when something as dumb and simple as an orange undergoes "the ordeal of expression"? he asks, his phrasing giving equal weight to two senses of "expression": "representation" and "squeezing." Unlike a sponge, he tells us (*éponge* in French; once more, the writer's own name is encrypted here), which gathers its form back again, the orange loses its. Its cells are crushed, its tissue ripped; there is spillage; but a husk remains; and, on the squeezer's part, a bitter sensation of seeds ejaculated too soon. The orange's facticity imposes itself on the expresser, yet can't be mastered or possessed by him—not empirically or mimetically or in any other way. Despite its debasing—indeed, in its very baseness—the orange, like Wallace Stevens's plum, "survives its poems." Stevens also turns to oranges, and in a surprisingly similar way: in "The Revolutionists Stop for Orangeade" the fruit becomes the pithy counterpoint to the regimented order of whatever ideology or program in whose name the soldiers march; an interruption that allows the intercession, as the poem's final couplet puts it,

Of the real that wrenches,
Of the quick that's wry.

V.

For Heidegger, drawing on Hölderlin, "poetically man dwells." In other words, poetry is not a representation of life, nor an embellishment of it, but rather the very mode and measure of our coming into being. Being, like poetry— or, rather, Being-as-poetry—entails a process of revealment (albeit one that unfolds in concealed form), through which reality is (to repeat the formulation I used earlier) brought forth or produced. To which we should add that this bringing-forth takes place, as the writers whom I've discussed here suggest time and again, in relation to a real that is resistant to this very process. I've spoken of this real in terms of trauma, and I've spoken of it in terms of matter— and it strikes me that in fact these aren't really two separate subjects or categories. For Freud, psychic trauma is a quite material phenomenon, for the good reason that the entire field of mental existence is a material one: by 1920, in *Beyond the Pleasure Principle*, he's winding every organism, ours included, back to its core status as "an undifferentiated vesicle of a substance that is susceptible to stimulation"; the central nervous system back to its core function as an "ectoderm" or outside skin that serves as "an organ for receiving stimuli" or "excitatory traces"; and he writes of embryology, of earliest marine life, germ-plasms and protozoa, ciliates and infusoria, storing and replaying "the history of the earth we live in and of its relation to the sun." Reprising these thoughts five years later in "A Note Upon The 'Mystic Writing-Pad,'" he describes "cathectic innervations" being "sent out and withdrawn in rapid periodic impulses"; describes how, jellyfish-like, "the unconscious stretches out feelers, through the medium of the system *Pcpt.-Cs.*, towards the external world and hastily withdraws them as soon as they have sampled the excitations coming from it." But what's most astonishing, for me, about these medusozoan images is the fact that Freud houses them in a longer meditation on a reusable notepad consisting of a "slab of dark brown resin or wax" over which lie, firstly, a layer of translucent waxed paper and, secondly and outermost, a transparent piece of celluloid, such that inscriptions may be both kept and (on the paper although not the dark brown slab) erased. This is his decisive model for consciousness and, ultimately, for life. We are all writing machines, jellyfish included. In fact, jellyfish especially.

VI.

I want to leave you with, for reasons that will be abundantly clear, a short sequence from what I think might be the great—or at least the most greatly overlooked—mid-twentieth-century British (or rather, once again, Scottish) novel. Early on in Alexander Trocchi's *Cain's Book*, the junky narrator embarks on a strangely Proustian sequence of perception and recall in which, watching a man urinating in a New York alley, he becomes

> like a piece of sensitive photographic paper, waiting passively to feel the shock of impression. And then I was quivering like a leaf, more precisely like a mute hunk of appetitional plasm, a kind of sponge in which the business

of being excited was going on, run through by a series of external stimuli: the lane, the man, the pale light, the lash of silver—at the ecstatic edge of something to be known.

Here is everything I've just been talking about: sponges; plasm; stimuli; the shock of impression; consciousness as photo-synthesis plus the reenactment of that primal trauma—all of which are brought into alignment and hypostatized by the act which is the actual and obsessive subject of Trocchi's book: namely, the act of writing. The sequence kicks off a second recall-loop, an analepsis to an Edinburgh pub into which the narrator once followed another man whom he'd seen slipping something glinting back into his pocket as he emerged from an earlier (or, if you like, more primal) alley, and the (very Heideggerian) image of the narrator's fingers following the outline of a woman's body carved by a blade in rough wood ("I hadn't known wood so intimately before")—a loop whose eventual folding back into the present dictates that the narrator take the urinating man back to the scow or barge on which he lives and sleep with him. Just prior to the seduction, he tells us of the first man pulsing through the second:

I experienced a sly female lust to be impregnated by, beyond words and in a mystical way to confound myself with, not the man necessarily, though that was part of the possibility, but the secrecy of his gesture.

Not to "capture" or "decode" the gesture: to *confound* himself with its *secrecy*. Revealed concealment. This confounding, and its replay in the present, Trocchi tells us, is not just an "act of remembrance" but also "a making of significance" that generates each "fact" as "a selected fiction, and I am the agent also of what is unremembered." The scow on which they make love floats on the "black ink" of the Atlantic; inside it there is virtually nothing: just a single bed, a coal stove, cupboard, dresser, chair and table—and a typewriter.

2014

Tristram Shandy
On Balls and Planes

I.

ALEX TROCCHI URGED aspiring writers to go off and spend a year playing pinball. I always thought this was very good advice; but I could never explain, even to myself, *why* it made such sense, until—

But this is a digression. Which, here (where? in this library in which I'm writing, or the sofa, bed or train you're reading on? or in the context of the contract that binds me to Vintage, you to Sterne, and all of us to some "place" of literary history? or maybe *here* can designate, more vaguely and more dauntingly, the constellations of ideas and propositions, counterintuitions, paradoxes, spatio-temporal conundrums, and so forth, that billow out, like so much ontic devilry, from Sterne's Pandora's box-like novel. We'll see...) —which, "here" (then), makes it a good place to start. *Tristram Shandy* is, of course, a book about digressions, a book *of* digressions—interruptions, divagations and departures, sidetracks and reroutings and just plain delays. As generation after generation of amused, bewildered or frustrated critics have pointed out, its eponymous protagonist, its supposed "hero," can't even get himself born until one-third of the way through; his naming takes us to the halfway point; and as for actually *doing* anything, or even being available, onstage, in case the right conditions for such doing should present themselves—forget it.

The only section of the novel in which Tristram does appear and play an active role is one huge, volume-long intermission, an entirely (even by the standards of this book) out-of-sequence travelogue in which the narrative digresses from its own digressive self, both taking and describing what, in modern parlance, we would call a road trip. Maybe *that's* the proper place for us to start, or restart. Doesn't Sterne suggest as much by planting, at that volume's outset, a road sign, recycled from Pliny, that reads: *Non enim excursus hic eius*—"For this is no excursion from it"—*sed opus ipsum est*—"but it is the thing itself"?

II.

So, off we go. In Volume VII, Tristram, suddenly middle-aged and on the run from Death, has hightailed it from England to the Continent. He travels to the South of France in rickety, defective *chaises*, along post roads—highways built principally for information's (rather than people's) conveyance. The roads are tolled; French law requires the traveler to downpay for each relay stage just prior to covering it. When Tristram changes plan and covers a stage by river, he still finds himself obliged to fork out to the king's coffers for the land route he has pre-announced but left untraveled—an affront that causes him to cry, with fantastically disingenuous indignation: "*Bon Dieu*! what, pay for the way I go! and for the way I do not go!"

Things get worse. Tristram realizes that he has left his "remarks," his notes (for he is fully conscious of his journey's literary end), inside a pocket in the lining of the broken carriage that he's just sold to a salvage-man or "vamping chaise-undertaker" (this morbid phrasing of professional title, you can be sure, is Sterne's own); racing to this vamper's house, he finds the scrolls knotted *en papillotes* in the man's wife's hair. More knots appear—in other women's hair, or in their clothes—as do more slits in fabric. There's an analepsis (within the larger prolepsis) to a trip Tristram made previously to the same region with his father and his uncle, whose remembering *as* he passes through the spot again gives rise to a self-conscious moment of narrative accretion, as when fabric folds and doubles on itself—which doubling is itself redoubled by a cutaway to Tristram-the-author sitting at a desk writing the whole experience up. The challenge that this last activity presents concerns him deeply: How, he asks a little later as he crosses Languedoc's rich plains, can writers transform landscape into language without being left with "a large plain upon their hands, which they know not what to do with?" It can be done, Tristram tells us—but not here: he'll publish his "PLAIN STORIES" elsewhere, at some future date. (He won't; Yorick will, and they'll be anything but plain).

A host of other incidents occur, and we should pay them all attention—the more so, the more trivial or disconnected they initially appear. For my money, the volume's most striking episode is a non-event: Tristram's aborted pilgrimage to Lyons Cathedral, to observe the movements of Lippius's famous clock. He has a mind unsuited to appreciation of mechanical movement, he tells us (equally disingenuously), before diverting our attention to a story of the paths and circuits "round, and round, and round the world" on which fate's cogs and levers lead two doomed lovers. Arriving at the cathedral where the clock is housed, he is informed that it is "all out of joints, and had not gone for some years." Never mind, he reasons: "I shall be able to give the world a better account of the clock in its decay, than I could have done in its flourishing condition—" Do we receive this account? Of course not.

III.

"All out of joints": the words that Tristram mangles here are Hamlet's, and they also concern time. His revamping of them sends us right back to the start of Volume I, in which his parents' coitus, his own moment of conception, is knocked off course by his mother's inquiry as to whether his father has remembered to wind up the family clock. Nor is her off-topic veering a one-way phenomenon: through "an unhappy association of ideas" derived from Walter's custom of fixing the house's timepieces on the same day as he attends to "some other little family concernments," Elizabeth (*née* Mollineux—her very name suggests cogged and conjoining mechanisms) habitually substitutes clocks for sex *and* sex for clocks, setting in place a two-way channel of association, a looping mental circuit of departure and return, part of a psychic orrery whose rules dictate that, whichever spot on a given orbit she's supposed to occupy, she'll actually be at the far point of that orbit's ellipse.

I like to think that Alan Moore and Dave Gibbons had this episode in mind when writing the scene in their graphic masterpiece *Watchmen* in which sex takes place on a bed across which watch parts have lain seconds earlier. But that's a digression too. For Tristram the "HOMUNCULUS," whose adult incarnation wishes—retroactively and vainly (and once more, of course, disingenuously too)—that conception had resulted in "the production of a rational Being," the "scatter[ing] and "dispers[al]" that this untimely outbreak of mental Copernicanism brings about proves fatal: the very sperm that might have produced such a being has been zapped, its DNA all scrambled, from the start; from this point on, all fixed points will be set in perpetual (and what's worse, *relative*) motion; all straight paths twisted and unraveled and reknotted into a freeway-junctionery of intersections, overlaps, and loopings. Tristram's thoughts will be not ratiocinated but (to borrow a term from Deleuze) rhizomatic; all his attempts to grapple with a given subject will be breached by endless detours through whole hosts of other subjects, histories, epistemologies; his entire life, far from progressing from one concrete event (and its interpretation) to the next, will consist of a sidereal slide through clusters of associations; Shandean time is metonymic, rather than metronomic, time.

As for the hero, so for the whole book: *Tristram Shandy* is a road-trip that goes everywhere and nowhere, in which vehicles as fast as Stevinus's legendary wind-powered land-yacht move alongside ones as slow as Yorick's dopey nag (not only *alongside*, but also, somehow, *at the same speed as*), across wormholed terrain that at one moment sends you on a four-year journey from Flanders to Yorkshire while two minutes, thirteen and three-fifths seconds simultaneously elapse, and, at the next one, bogs you down ("the country thereabouts being nothing but a deep clay") in quagmires that keep two characters frozen in mid-gesture for ten chapters. Tristram's "proper" name, his intended one of Trismegistus, carries implicitly, through its derivation from the mythic Hermes Trismegistus, an allusion to the god of routes and wayfarers; also of messages—for roads are always postroads, just as narrative, like man himself, is (as Sterne reminds us constantly) a "vehicle." And none of these will ever move in a straight line: "Could a historiographer drive on his history, as a muleteer drives on his mule,—straight forward..." Tristram muses wistfully; "but the thing is, morally speaking, impossible: For, if he is a man of the least spirit, he will have fifty deviations from a straight line to make with that or that party as he goes along..." Typographically, lines give over to wandering graphemes that recall musical notation, or Paul Klee's characterization of drawing as "taking a line for a walk" (a line that, like a dog, must meander off to sniff behind each hedge, piss on each lamppost, and chase after every tail, its own included); structurally, they give over to a series of "adventitious parts" with "intersections" so "involved... one wheel within another" that "the machinery of my work" becomes "a species by itself; two contrary motions are introduced into it, and reconciled, which were thought to be at variance with each other. In a word, my work is digressive, and it is progressive too."

IV.

All that would be fine; we would have a complex, but manageable, book, a Newtonian (or even, *avant-la-lettre*, Einsteinean) novel in which thoughts and events, well calibrated, counterbalance one another, held together by a narrative force field that confers equilibrium on the whole. We *would*, were it not for one thing: error. Walter knows this all too well. He dreams of such a novel—dreams of life *as* such a novel. "To come at the exact weight of things in the scientific steel-yard, the fulcrum, he would say, should be almost invisible.... Knowledge, like matter, he would affirm, was divisible *in infinitum*;—that the grains and scruples were as much a part of it, as the gravitation of the whole world." Yet when error worms its way into this system, "no matter where it fell,—whether in a fraction,—or a pound,—'twas alike fatal to truth, and she was kept down at the bottom of her well, as inevitably by a mistake in the dust of a butterfly's wing,—as in the disk of the sun, the moon, and all the stars of heaven put together."

Error is everywhere in *Tristram Shandy*; it's the most

glitch-ridden book imaginable—it's *all* glitch. Everything gets lost or misdirected; every action generates unwanted consequences. For the system-elaborating Walter, Tristram represents no more or less than the disaster zone in which all systems are undone; in the travails Sterne heaps with almost sadistic pleasure on the boy, Walter sees "my system turned topside-turvy," the "fine network of the intellectual web" that he feels is man's due get "rent and torn." "Unhappy Tristram! child of wrath! child of decrepitude! interruption! mistake! and discontent! What one misfortune or disaster in the book of embryotic evils, that could unmechanize thy frame, or entangle thy filaments! which has not fallen upon thy head…" Tristram may be more prone to catastrophe than most; but, as with all literary heroes who stand at the extreme end of some scale or other, we soon come to realize that, far from being exceptional, he is in fact simply *more* normal than everybody else (Freud would say the same of neurotics and even psychotics). The evil that befalls Tristram is a general one: as Walter wailingly acknowledges, all heads, every "seat of the understanding," must pass through a wrongly shaped crack in order to be brought into the world. Don't underestimate the role of gender here: within the Shandean universe, system is male, error is female. It's the gap, the slit, the tear, that breaks into and interrupts that universe's carefully elaborated structure, the unmeasurable delay that, like Penelope confounding all her suitors, unravels its finely woven fabric. Error is universal, and all men are Tristrams.

And yet Sterne is too wise to take at face value the conventional misogyny of this formulation. Walter's system may be elaborate, but its own fulcrum, its "treasury" and "canon's prayer book," resides in the many tomes of Hafen Slawkenbergius—a made-up polymath whose name means "Chamberpot Pile of Offal": Walter, Sterne informs us through the cover of a Germano-Latin compound, is full of shit. And even if he weren't, a more essential problem undermines all system-building—an inherent, rather than external (as is error), one. In an aside that, naturally, isn't an aside at all, Tristram muses that, all fruits in "this great harvest of our learning" having ripened over centuries and now nearing that apex at which *all* will be known:

> When that happens, it is to be hoped, it will put an end to all kind of writings whatsoever;—the want of all kind of writing will put an end to all kind of reading;—and that in time, *As war begets poverty; poverty, peace,*—must, in course, put an end to all kind of knowledge,—and then—we shall have to begin all over again; or, in other words, be exactly where we started.

Here, Sterne seems to anticipate Hegel's Total System—and its collapse. Rather than lead in a straight upward line towards pure Spirit, the path Tristram envisages for thought and history (or history-as-thought and thought-as-history) twists round in a Viconian *ricorso*, as progress gives way to repetition.

Error from without; error from within. Even the hero's name is wrong. In her transit from the hallway to the bedroom, Susannah tongue-ties *Trismegistus* into a garble of *Tris*-somethings from which the curate extracts *Tristram*. This one, we could say, is a meta-error, a recursive one: Susannah, playing the role of Hermes, has lost Hermes himself in the post, in the "delivery." Message relay is overtaken by a melancholia, a *tristesse*, that eats at it from the inside, twists it from its path. To put it in the thermo-cybernetic language that one of Sterne's obvious descendants, Thomas Pynchon, would attach to his creation Tristero (*Trisheros* and *Tiriseroe*, incidentally, are associates or variants of *Trismegistus*), information is beset with entropy. This, perhaps, is why Aunt Dinah looms so large and awkwardly within the Shandy family memory: she, like her biblical counterpart, and like all the other contents of this novel's *post-chaises*, got screwed *en route*. If the specter of illegitimacy hovers, invisible and unspoken, over the Shandy family, the one surface on which it does write itself out large and fully legible is that of the family coach, across whose side the bungling painter has flipped *bend-dexter* into *bend-sinister* (once more, a drawn line gone AWOL). Narrative, in this book, is a vehicle, and, conversely, all vehicles denote narrative (as surely as clocks denote sex and vice versa): what's *really* illegitimate is not so much Tristram (although this is possible) as the narrative itself. Tristram's continental *chaise*, let's not forget, breaks down completely: having started out avowing his intent "to come at the first springs of the events I tell," Tristram ends up stranded at the wayside, the broken springs of the carriage shock-absorbers strewn out all around him. We have Klee's wandering line in mind already; but perhaps an even better template twentieth-century visual art could lend our understanding of this book might be Ed Ruscha's *Royal Road Test*, in which the parts of a typewriter that has been flung from a speeding car are repeatedly photographed scattered about the tarmac. Ruscha's choice of brand (Royal was a leading typewriter manufacturer) is not coincidental, any more than Sterne's mention of the regal nature of Tristram's relay-stage creditor in Volume VII is superfluous. All roads are post roads, and all post roads are the king's; but, in Sterne as much as Ruscha, what we witness, again and again, is a certain form of royalty or "sovereignty"—of the self, of writing—being taken apart, un-jointed.

"I shall be able to give the world a better account of the clock in its decay, than I could have done in its flourishing condition—" The entire text of *Tristram Shandy* is, in effect, that account. Reading it, we encounter, even at the level of the sentence, mechanisms collapsing into one another, a kind of literary autophagia. Take the passage in which Walter, having had his previous discourse interrupted by the breaking of his pipe (an instance of *Apesiopesis*, Tristram helpfully informs us), tries to explain to Toby another rhetorical device, ANALOGY, the context of their dialogue implicitly linking both these tropes with female sexual anatomy—when:

> a devil of a rap at the door snapped my father's definition (like his tobacco pipe) in two,—and, at the same time, crushed the head of as notable and curious a dissertation as ever was engendered in the womb of speculation.

Tristram's head is, at this very minute, being crushed in its passage from the womb. Action becomes figure; figure becomes object; object becomes correlative to action, all at once. Or the passage in which Toby's removal of his handkerchief from his coat pocket leads into a digression on the action's ergonomics, whose "transverse zigzaggery" recalls in Toby's mind the angles of the ramparts of Namur, which in turn leads Sterne into a digression on reviewers (in order to preemptively defend himself against attacks from these brought on by this last digression), and the body/soul divide (and here the craft of tailoring, whence the sequence took off, re-embeds itself as a conceit), and then blood circulation, which, like circulating blood itself, flows back round to the spot it left a microsecond—or eternity—ago. Nothing—and everything—has happened. More importantly, Trocchi's hermetic counsel starts to make sense, as we observe the exhilarating spectacle of language turning into a pinball machine, with buffers firing off to other buffers, ramps leading from one level to the next and counter-ramps plunging two levels down, holes swallowing balls up and shooting them out elsewhere as lights flash, bells *ping!* and the whole contraption shifts into multi-ball mode. We watch this with exhilaration, and with vertigo as well—because we know, like Walter and like Tristram too, that gravity, or Death, will make all balls come crashing down eventually.

V.

Comedy, as Bergson (whose ideas of *durée* are so perfectly foreshadowed by Sterne's own) tells us, consists of the transformation of unique or "natural" life into mechanisms that engender repetition. For Baudelaire, it turns around the pratfall or the simple act of falling—that is, around gravity, and, by extension, the grave towards which all things fall. For Paul de Man, it resides in an awareness of inauthenticity whose consequences, ultimately, are anything but funny. "The moment the innocence or authenticity of our sense of being in the world is put into question," he writes, "a far from harmless process gets underway. It may start as a casual bit of play with a stray loose end of the fabric, but before long the entire texture of the self is unravelled and comes apart."

The pertinence of these conjectures to this book of mechanisms, repetitions and unravelings, this book whose last word goes to the namesake and descendant of Hamlet's death's-head comedian Yorick ("he had," Sterne tells us of his pastor, "an invincible dislike and opposition in his nature to gravity;—not to gravity as such;—for where gravity was wanted, he would be the most grave or serious of mortal men for days and weeks together...")—this goes without saying. But what of comedy's close neighbor, nonsense? For Deleuze, who has already lent us his rhizomes, *non-sens* should be understood in its most literal sense of "not-direction"; that is, as lacking any singular direction—or, as Sterne would put it, driven (or riven) by contrary pulls and motions. Clearly, the definition is equally pertinent here. Even in terms of the word's common usage, there are sequences of *Tristram Shandy* that are utterly nonsensical, that wouldn't be out of place in Lewis Carroll or Edward Lear. In the long, parable-like tales of noses and of whiskers, for example, it becomes less and less clear what *nose* or *whisker* might actually *mean*. The very word is (as Sterne puts it) "ruined"; its own use has "given it a wound"; like Tristram's head, "not the better for passing through all these defiles," it is defiled. And this defiling leads to general semantic entropy:

> Does not all the world know, said the curate d'Estella at the conclusion of his work, that Noses ran the same fate some centuries ago in most parts of Europe, which Whiskers have now done in the kingdom of Navarre?—The evil indeed spread no further then—but have not beds and bolsters, and nightcaps and chamber-pots stood upon the brink of destruction ever since? Are not trouse, and placket-holes, and pump-handles—and spigots and faucets, in danger still from the same association?

Joyce, another obvious heir to Tristram's woes, will write in (and of) *Finnegans Wake*:

> in the Nichtian glossery which purveys aprioric roots for aposteriorious tongues this is nat language in any sinse of the world and one might as fairly go and kish his sprogues as fail to certify whether the wartrophy eluded

at some lives earlier was that somethink like a jug, to
what, a coctable

Sterne's book, too, is a Nichtian glossery, in which language's
power to designate objects, to represent the world, becomes
increasingly eroded. Its author may heap scorn on theolo-
gians who debate whether or not a child can be baptized
before even the tiniest part of him has emerged from the
womb; but this masks his genuine concern about the possibility (or otherwise) of naming *tout court*. How, and at
what point, he wonders, should an orator pull from beneath
his cloak the object of his oratory, be this "a scar, an axe, a
sword, a pink'd doublet, a rusty helmet, a pound and a half
of pot-ashes in an urn, or a three-halfpenny pickle pot"—or,
indeed, a baby? Keep the last of these concealed for too long
and "it must certainly have beshit the orator's mantle."
Things and events, like babies or even fetuses, need to receive
the sacrament of language, to be rendered clean and visible
by it. Would for biographers that we lived on Mercury,
whose heat would just turn everything into "one fine transparent body of clear glass"! But, alas, we live on Earth, and
Earth is made of mud. The countryside around Shandy Hall
must be rivaled only by Dickens's Thames Estuary as the
muddiest landscape in all literature: a "mire," an "explosion
of mud," a "majesty of mud," "a vortex of mud and water."

Yorick's sermon on Conscience spends ten days buried in mud; learned men are pictured "rolling one over the other" in it...

VI.

Plain tales, tales of mud. How do you write about a life, redeem a murky, tangled event-landscape into clarity and truth? Uncle Toby, in his own, untutored manner, dedicates his life to just this question. Having been wounded in the groin within the ravelins and ditches, trenches, dykes and counterscarps of Namur, then mired down all over again in his attempts to tell of it ("by Heaven; his life was put in jeopardy by words"), he ends up representing the whole muddy episode not in language, but in mud itself. His bowling-garden being full of nature's "kindliest compost... with just so *much* clay in it, as to retain the form of angles and indentings,—and so *little* of it too, as not to cling to the spade," he has his man Trim sculpt it, first into a scale model of Namur's citadel, then into one of every fortified, besieged town that he can find a map of. This is his mute, looping, spring-like answer to the straight line of conventional wisdom: willed repetition in the form of reenactment. Just as Ballard's anti-hero Vaughan will, two hundred years later, restage car crashes (first his own and then everyone else's, until the hybrid or generic car crash becomes elevated to the status of a universal situation), Toby restages battles. This gives him "intense pleasure" even as it replays a scene of immense and ongoing pain. In doing so, it illustrates to a *t*—and once again *avant la lettre*—Freud's theory of trauma, which is also linked to repetition. And if Pynchon's Tristero might—maybe—owe something to Tristram's lost name, then his Slothrop (*his* name, let's note, is bookended by *Slop*), whose groin has also been indelibly marked by projectiles and their parabolas, must *surely* be Toby's bastard descendant.

Is Toby simply marked, or has he been castrated? This is what Widow Wadman wants to know. The former, Trim assures the widow's servant Bridget, as she "hold[s] the palm of her left hand parallel to the plane of the horizon, and slid[es] the fingers of the other over it, in a way which could not have been done, had there been the least wart or protuberance"—but in the battlefield of public rumor, it's the latter. And his reenactments themselves cause the ur-episode of pubic wounding to spring back into action all over again, replaying itself this time on Tristram's body. The sash window through which Tristram unwisely urinates (like Mercury's putative Momus-glass, a vitreous lens through which the world might be viewed clearly—first posited, then brought crashing down) falls on his penis because Trim has commandeered its weights and pulleys for the garden's model cannons. Rumor also has it that Tristram has been castrated; in fact, he ends up merely circumcised (a fulfillment-by-typo of his earlier wish to become "a being guarded and circum-scribed with rights")—but, as with Toby, rumor's knife cuts off the whole caboodle; and, for good measure, Sterne's pen slices in with a litany of variants on cuts and cutting as Trim, making a circumcising gesture, recalls members of Cutts's regiment getting "all cut to pieces." Circumscription be-comes circumcision becomes castration.

For Freud, the symbolic castration cut into the body by the circumcising ritual represents the male child's passage into the symbolic order. Lacan takes this further: for him, castration is this order's secret truth. Sterne is a Lacanian, right down to the level of typography: cuts or omissions, in the form of dashes, form the basic building block of every page. If castration is the symbolic order's truth, then it is also that of writing, "wounded" or "cock-and-bull" language that, unable to inseminate the world with meaning, can do no more than reinscribe this truth recursively. Tristram him-self adds the chapter on weights and sashes to his father's *Tristapedia*, filling in for what's been cut from it with an account of cutting—his own—itself.

VII.

As Plato founded his Republic on the exclusion of poets, F. R. Leavis built the system of his Great Tradition on the relegation of *Tristram Shandy* to a footnote, its dismissal as "irresponsible" and "trifling." I could counter (after noting the irony that no one under forty will have heard of F. R. Leavis, let alone have read his now largely out-of-print books) by claiming that Sterne's novel is in fact the cornerstone of all serious (though that would be the wrong word) literature that followed, right down to the present day (which Yorick's skull is David Foster Wallace really digging up in *Infinite Jest*, for example?), or some such. The assertion might not be *wrong*, but I feel that it would miss the point. In a way, conservatives like Leavis are right: *Tristram Shandy* is, and will continue to be, the unraveling of any systematic or linear account of literature we might come up with. It is more than just an instance of great writing; it's a mise-en-scène of writing's very condition: joyous, anguished, vertiginous and ultra-paradoxical—and that of life: a gap, or slit, or pocket in which spinning bodies, held up, despite all odds, in a miasma of impossibility, career for an indefinite interval across a tilted plane before heading to the floor. *Kerthunk.*

2013

Recessional, or the Time of the Hammer

TOWARDS THE END of Thomas Pynchon's mammoth 1973 novel *Gravity's Rainbow*, the stumbling ingénue of a hero Tyrone Slothrop sets off on a commando-raid. The territory he and his cohorts move through is a giant metropolis, a "factory-state" in which capital, technology and power, perfectly co-calibrated, send airships drifting through urban canyons, past chrome caryatids and roof-gardens on skyscrapers that themselves shoot up and down on elevator-cables: a conurbation Pynchon calls the "City of the Future" or "Raketen-Stadt." The raid's target, though, is not a building; nor is it a person; it is, rather, time. Slothrop has been dispatched to rescue "the Radiant Hour," which associates of a villain known only as "the Father" have "abstracted from the day's 24." As Slothrop, suiting up and setting out, is handed a note informing him, in matinee adventure style: "The Radiant Hour is being held captive, if you want to see her...," the bullets zinging past his head "conveniently" give over to a clock face, drifting, like the airships, through the sky.

How do we digest or get a bearing on this bizarre episode? The fact that one of the "Floundering Four" commandos is a "very serious-looking French refugee kid" named Marcel, "a mechanical chess-player dating back to the Second Empire" given to long-winded monologues, might point us towards Proust, inviting us to view Slothrop's escapade as a reworking of that other raid on lost (or misappropriated) time, stage-managed by a writer who has put something extra in his *madeleines*. The intention was probably there on Pynchon's part—yet as I re-read the sequence a few weeks ago, my mind kept drifting (maybe it was the Franco-Germanic mix of Marcel and Raketen-Stadt, the general elevation of the setting) to another scene, another half-occluded precedent; one that plays out in Switzerland.

Thomas Mann's equally mammoth work *The Magic Mountain* announces, right from the outset, an obsession with time. As Hans Castorp (another ingénue protagonist) winds his way up through mountains to the Davos sanatorium to visit his tubercular cousin, the space through which his train chuffs starts to take on "the powers we generally ascribe to time." Numerous temporal meditations follow—on duration, on persistence, continuity, recurrence. As though foreseeing that Davos would become the seat of the

World Economic Forum, Mann has one of Hans's teachers, Naphta, explain the global financial market to him as a temporally-grounded system, a mechanism for "receiving a premium for the passage of time—interest, in other words." At the outset of a chapter titled "By the Ocean of Time," the form and very possibility of the book we are reading become similarly index-linked to time, "For time is the medium of narration." "Can one tell—that is to say, narrate—time, time itself, as such, for its own sake?" Mann wonders. No: "That would surely be an absurd undertaking." Yet he concedes that any narrative contains two kinds of time: that of its actual time, the time it takes to iterate itself; and that of its content, which is "extremely relative," such that a narrative that concerned itself with the events of five minutes might take up hundreds of hours, and, conversely, the contents of a moment's iteration might expand beyond "the extreme limit of man's temporal capacity for experience." The latter, expansive instances, he claims, are possessed of "a morbid element" and are akin to opium dreams in which "something had been taken away" from the brain of the sleeper, "like the spring from a broken watch."

Hans plans to stay at the sanatorium for three weeks; but, himself diagnosed with TB on arrival, is held up there for seven years. His illness not only forces an extended delay, time off from his work as an engineer, a general time-out from his life; it also imposes its own temporality. When you are ill in bed, Mann writes,

> All the days are nothing but the same day repeating itself—or rather, since it is always the same day, it is incorrect to speak of repetition; a continuous present, an identity, an everlastingness—such words as these would better convey the idea. They bring you your midday broth, as they brought it yesterday and will bring it tomorrow; and it comes over you—but whence or how you do not know, it makes you quite giddy to see the broth coming in—that you are losing a sense of the demarcation of time, that its units are running together, disappearing; and what is being revealed to you as the true content of time is merely a dimensionless present in which they eternally bring you the broth.

Colored by shades of eternity and entropy or run-down, illness-time is time that is drifting towards death. But it is also, in classic Freudian fashion, time that is homing in on pleasure. Illness "makes men more physical," Mann notes; racking women's frames, consumption brings about a "heightening and accentuation" of their curves and outlines, turns them into beings "exaggerated by disease and rendered twice over body." "Pthisis and concupiscence go together," remarks Dr. Behrens, while his colleague Dr. Krokowski talks of love, forced underground by "fear, conventionality, aversion, or a tremulous yearning to be pure," reemerging "in the form of illness. Symptoms of disease are nothing but a disguised manifestation of the power of love; and all disease is only love transformed."

These lines of thought play out dramatically (as those of you who have read the book will know) in the relation between Hans and fellow patient Clavdia Chauchat (her name, beside denoting femininity and lust, is also that of a make of machine-gun). Hans experiences his desire for her as an extension and intensification of his illness. In a gesture that redeems a romantic cliché by literalizing it, Mann has Hans's temperature, constantly thermometer-gauged, rise two notches every time he sees her; and, in a similar materialization of chivalric code, he makes him carry around an X-ray of her lungs, pressed tight against his chest: thus she becomes, like Pynchon's stolen hour, both radiant and negative, abstracted. Though she remains beyond his reach for virtually the whole novel, he mounts a seduction in the book's central episode, which takes place on Walpurgis Night—a festival or holiday abstracted even from the abstracted life of the sanatorium, time out of the time-out ("almost," as Hans puts it, "outside the calendar, intercalated, so to speak, a twenty-ninth of February"). The seduction sequence begins with him reenacting (unbeknown to Clavdia) another episode that shaped his childhood when, aged thirteen, he borrowed a pencil from a boy on whom he had a crush. Recalling the childhood incident earlier in the novel has already caused him to be rapt back into the past "so strongly, so resistlessly" that his present body has seemed like that of a cadaver "while the actual Hans Castorp moved in that far-away time and place"; replaying it on Walpurgis Night as he asks Clavdia for her pencil places him, once more, "on the tiled court of the schoolyard."

Thus a complex, spring-like structure opens up, stretching and contracting such that quite separate moments touch or get embedded one within the other, with a synecdoche or marker for the act of writing (the pencil) running through it all. Lavishing praise on Clavdia's flesh "*destinée pour l'anatomie du tombeau*," Hans asks to die with his lips pressed to hers. Most commentaries on *The Magic Mountain* interpret the fact that Clavdia leaves the party at this point as a rebuff; yet her words in the doorway—"*N'oubliez pas de me rendre mon crayon*"—Hans's pointedly late return to his own room, and Mann's mention of more words exchanged between them that night at "a later interval, wordless to our ears, during which we have elected to intermit the flow of our story along the stream of time, and let time flow on pure and free of any content whatever" strongly suggest the opposite. If it is the writing implement that opens the approach to death-like pleasure up, though, it is the same one that, in Mann's hands, places its consummation in a blind spot. Either way, content-time kicks back in the next day, and Clavdia leaves, returning much later as the companion of the older Mynheer Peeperkorn, who, standing between Hans and her, becomes one more of Hans's surrogate fathers. Peeperkorn will commit suicide, while Hans, discharged, is sent off to the front of World War I, as the novel's ironic ending sees the long, intimate, death-like intermission of the sanatorium give over to the wholesale mechanized slaughter of historical progression.

HANS CASTORP, of course, isn't the only literary hero with TB. We could all probably name a handful of writers who succumbed to it, and scores more characters. One of this second group whose story doesn't get discussed so much these days, not least because of the racist epithet in its title, is the hero of Joseph Conrad's novella *The Nigger of the "Narcissus."* The setting (for those of you who need reminding) is a British Merchant vessel sailing back to London from Bombay—a little world, just like Mann's sanatorium, with its hierarchies and operational rhythms, isolated from the larger one it micro-mirrors, set this time at a degree zero of elevation, on a literal ocean. As the first mate calls the roster prior to casting off, and notes that they are one man short (there is an extra name written down there, but he can't make it out; it is smudged), he is about to dismiss the crew when a voice calls out: "Wait!" The mate, incensed by the insubordination, demands to know who dared to tell *him* to wait—whereupon a black man steps out of the shadows, a West Indian sailor named James Wait.

No sooner has Wait announced his presence than a cough leaps from him, "metallic, hollow, and tremendously loud; it resounded like two explosions in a vault; the dome of the sky ran to it, and the iron plates of the ship's bulwarks seemed to vibrate in unison." He will spend most of the trip laid up with his coughing; on the rare occasions when he steps out on deck, "a black mist emanated from him ... something cold and gloomy that floated out and settled on all the faces like a mourning veil." Conrad heaps funereal symbols (corpses, coffins, shrouds) upon Wait; and Wait welcomes the association, telling the crew he is dying at every opportunity, even seeming "to take a pride in that death." "He would," writes Conrad, "talk of that coming death as though it had been already there, as if it had been walking the deck outside, as if it would presently come in to sleep in the only empty bunk; as if it had sat by his side at every meal." The effect on the crew is complex. Wait's morbidity fills them with trepidation, while his black face repulses them. At the same time, his plight awakens their humanity. They indulge him; cover for him; bring him meals, even plunder the ship's supplies to pander to him. Before long, they become loyal yet dread-filled servants, "the base courtiers of a hated prince." The forecastle in which they lodge him turns into a "church" where men, entering, speak only "in low tones"—or, in more pagan shades, a "shrine where a black idol, reclining stiffly under a blanket, blinked its weary eyes and received our homage." "He had the secret of life, that confounded dying man, and he made himself master of every moment of our existence."

But is he genuine? In an exchange with his fellow crew member Donkin, a work-shy syndicalist whose shirking has nothing of the metaphysical about it (Conrad's novella is decidedly not tailored to a liberal readership), Wait admits to "shamming" his sickness in order to obtain an easy passage. And yet even as he speaks the words, more coughs rattle his by-now skeletal frame. When the captain accuses him of shamming too (as it turns out, from compassion—he, like the rest of them, can see that Wait is doomed), Wait claims to have recovered; the captain confines him to his forecastle, and the crew almost mutiny. Yet the stand-off seems more philosophical than political: Wait's "steadfast-ness to his untruthful attitude" (a double-edged term, since Wait is lying twice over: lying about being well, and lying about lying in the first place) "in the face of the inevitable truth had," writes Conrad, "the proportions of a colossal enigma." The whole ship teeters on the edge of an abysmal ambiguity; "nothing in her was real." It drifts into the dol-drums, which (since it is sail-powered) delays its onward passage—a hiatus that seems to affirm that "The universe conspired with James Wait," since he, too, as he drifts deathwards, is borne into "regions of memory that know nothing of time." "There was," writes Conrad, "something of the immutable quality of eternity in the slow moments of his complete restfulness." And, as in *The Magic Mountain*, lurking somewhere in the depths of this un-clockworked death-space is a half-buried scene of sexual pleasure: in his delirium, Wait mumbles about a "Canton Street girl . . . She chucked a third engineer of a Rennie boat . . . for me. Cooks oysters just as I like . . ."

After he finally dies and disappears, canvas-wrapped, into the sea, the wind picks up and the *Narcissus* speeds onwards to London. The last scene sees the crew collect their pay (Wait's own salary, since he has no claimants, is put aside, retained) in the shipping company's office just beside the Royal Mint—for a merchant ship's passage is, after and above all, a move in the great monetary game of industry and trade. Yet, under the name of Wait, a dark aporia has opened up somewhere inside the game-space; a suspension or negation of its logic; a threat, or at least the kernel of one, to its very continuation.

As I wrote this essay, I kept hearing a tune playing in my head, as you do. It was a particular tune, repeating over and over again: MC Hammer's "U Can't Touch This." You know the one: it is built around a single four-beat musical phrase that loops round and round, while MC Hammer overlays the verbal phrases "U can't touch this" and "Stop! Hammertime." How logical is the Unconscious. This was no random, meaningless distraction: the song couldn't have been more germane to the thoughts I was trying to piece together—for doesn't it, like Conrad's novella, feature a black man who tells us to wait? A little detective work, the kind you can easily do on Wikipedia, reveals the repeating tune to already be a repetition: MC Hammer has sampled it from Rick James's "Superfreak," removing James's lyrics ("She's a very kinky girl / The kind you don't take home to mother") and inserting his refrain "U can't touch this" in the little pause, the suspended beat that opens just before the tune loops round again. We get this opening refrain three times; then, in the "break-down" coda separating one verse from the next, its rejoinder: "Stop! Hammertime"—as though, just like Wait, Hammer were baptizing the hiatus with his own name.

CONRAD'S NOVELLA was first published, in 1897, with a preface that is generally taken as the author's overriding literary manifesto. Drawing an analogy between the manual laborer and the writer, Conrad calls the latter a "worker in prose"—but, counterintuitively, links the great literary work not to a labor's successful completion, but rather to its suspension. "To arrest, for the space of a breath, the hands busy about the work of the earth, and compel men entranced by the sight of distant goals to glance for a moment at the surrounding vision of form and color, of sunshine and shadows; to make them pause for a look, for a sigh, for a smile—such is the aim, difficult and evanescent, and reserved only for a very few to achieve." *Arrest* and *pause* are the key terms here; also *reserved*, which conveys the sense of some great bounty or reward that, like Wait's salary (or Clavdia, or the

Radiant Hour), has been withheld, removed to a location beyond normal reach. Conrad's preface, for all its talk of pauses and arrests, is equally spatial: the writer "descends within himself, and in that lonely region of stress and strife, if he be deserving and fortunate, he finds the terms of his appeal." That the descent into and re-emergence from this dark region "binds the dead to the living" by holding up a "rescued fragment" of truth to the light gives it a thoroughly Orphic character—and turns the entire preface, for me, into a kind of dry run for that seminal twentieth-century literary manifesto that Maurice Blanchot would publish fifty years later under the title "The Gaze of Orpheus." I have written about this at some length elsewhere, so will confine myself to noting here that Blanchot carries Conrad's motifs of arrest and incompletion one step further: what's remarkable about Orpheus, he points out, is not that he manages to rescue the lost radiant object, but that (in looking back) he interrupts and vandalizes even his own labor, bringing back to the light not Eurydice's presence but rather her absence.

This logic of the negative pervades all Blanchot's work. As though also thinking of "hands busy about the work of the earth," he writes: "Take the trouble to listen to a single word: in that word, nothingness is struggling and toiling away, it digs tirelessly, doing its best to find a way out, nullifying what encloses it"—this in an essay called "Literature and the Right to Death." No writer is more death-obsessed than Blanchot; and, for him, death is intimately tied in with the question of time. His short novella *Death Sentence*, also utterly Orphic, narrates an encounter between a man and his dead female friend whose corpse he visits, during which visit, despite remaining quite dead, she sits up and chats casually with him—for a while. Its original French title, *L'Arrêt de Mort*, contains the double sense of a condemnation *and* a temporary reprieve or suspension (an *arrête*), as though the judge's hammer hovered in mid-air above its block. His later, autobiographical essay *L'Instant de ma Mort* recounts his experience of facing a firing squad during the Second World War—feeling, despite everything, a rush of joy as the soldiers, "in an immobility that arrested time," pointed their guns at him; then, when the actual shooting inexplicably failed to happen (he would live another sixty years), a perpetual sense of carrying "the instant of my death henceforth always in abeyance"—*L'instant de ma mort désormais toujours en instance*. Writing of death elsewhere, he distinguishes *la mort*, death itself, from *mourir*, dy-*ing*: where the first would be a thing that one could grasp, experience, consume (an unrealizable fantasy—yet one that underlies the entire tragic and Romantic literary traditions), the second is a neutral, uncontainable, unmasterable drifting, a movement of absenting. Thus, for the Blanchot of *The Writing of the Disaster*, dying is the opposite of death: it is "the incessant imminence whereby life lasts, desiring."

Dy-*ing*, desir-*ing*: in grammatical terms, these non-finite verbs belong to the gerund—the form that, in English, also serves as the present participle. The tense, if you like, of Hans Castorp's eternally arriving soup. Or, to take another high-modernist literary instance, of Addie Bundren's passage through the novel whose very title contains Blanchot's gerund: *As I Lay Dying*. This work contains or concentrates so many of the processes and motifs we've been looking at here. Not only does Addie, like Wait, slowly and languorously die, but the hiatus mushrooms outwards even after the death-moment: while her family transport her coffin to the burial place she has stipulated, encountering delays at every step, the corporeality that Mann associates with illness is taken to its own zero-degree as her rotting corpse draws buzzards from the sky and sends townspeople running gagging from its path. Advancing "with a motion so soporific, so dreamlike as to be uninferant of progress," the family edges towards a flooded river, and Addie's son Darl muses, in a gesture that will be familiar: "It is as though the space between us were time: an irrevocable quality." He continues: "It is as though time, no longer running straight before us in a diminishing line, now runs parallel between us like a looping string, the distance being the doubling accretion of the thread." It is into this accretion that Addie's body threatens to disappear as the flood waters sweep the coffin from the cart. But Darl rescues it—and a few pages later, in the novel's most stunning sequence, Faulkner gives the dead Addie her own monologue; Eurydice, rather than Orpheus, speaks.

She speaks both in and of the negative. "I learned," she says, "that words are no good; that words don't ever fit even what they are trying to say at." Even the word *love* "is just a shape to fill a lack." Lying beside her husband Anse, who has tricked her by hiding inside that last word,

> I would think about his name until after a while I could see the word as a shape, a vessel, and I would watch him liquefy and flow into it like cold molasses flowing out of the darkness into the vessel, until the jar stood full and motionless: a significant shape profoundly without life like an empty door frame; and then I would find that I had forgotten the name of the jar.

Anse is, she tells us, dead; her revenge on him consists in not letting him know that, and her marital bond in the fact "that I did not even ask him for what he could have given me: not-Anse. That was my duty to him, to not ask that, and that duty I fulfilled. I would be I; I would let him be the shape and echo of his word." Her affair with the pastor Whitfield is conducted largely in the hope that the Christian schema of sin and subsequent redemption will act as a funnel "to shape and coerce" the "terrible blood" of existence into a form of presence and equivalence, but since divinity itself is just "the forlorn echo of the dead word high in the air" (and "salvation is just words too"), the affair ends—which places her inside a kind of timelessness in which "to me there was no beginning nor ending to anything." And occupying this space, this temporality, she tells us in a fascinating turn of phrasing, "I even held Anse refraining still, not that I was holding him recessional..."

These words need some unpacking. *Refraining* is the more straight-forward: I take it to mean that she is holding herself back from revealing Anse to himself as the not-Anse that, to her, he more profoundly is—maintaining him, to use the kind of photographic diction X-ray-clasping Hans Castorp might understand, in false-positive mode by keeping out of sight the actual negative from which this positive is (again and again, an ongoing illusion) printed. *Recessional* is more complex though. The OED gives *recessional* as: "1. Of or belonging to the recession or retirement of the clergy and choir from the chancel to the vestry at the close of a service; esp. *recessional hymn*, a hymn sung while this retirement is taking place. 2. Belonging to a recess (of Parliament)."

Recess, in turn, is given (inter alia) as "The act of retiring, withdrawing, or departing...a period of cessation from usual work or employment...a place of retirement, a remote, secret or private place...a niche or alcove...to place in a recess or in retirement; to set back or away..." It is a long entry, spanning architectural, juridical, anatomical and a host of other contexts—not least economic (aren't we now living through a recession?). If Addie *is* holding Anse refraining, *recessional* describes the manner in which she is *not* holding him, names the inner sanctum into which she is denying him entry (can't touch this), the time-out-of-time that will never be measured on his clock-face, governed by his legislature—and, in so doing, names the suspended or abstracted beat around whose absence the whole mechanism of the book is orchestrated. *As I Lay Dying*, for all its entropy and breakdown, is a neatly circular novel in which all actions come back round as the cycle of life rotates: Addie's son Cash breaks the same leg twice, her daughter Dewey Dell gets screwed over (or screwed) twice, and so forth; and Anse, in the final punchline, marries the woman from whom he borrowed the spade he has just dug Addie's grave with. The corpse may be disposed of, the cycle restarted, but the recess has staked its claim right at its core, carved out its niche at twelve o'clock of midnight and high noon.

A PATTERN IS, I hope, emerging here. If I have been drawing on works that, despite their evident preoccupation with issues of race and gender, were all authored by white men, this is not simply from a placid conservatism. Rather, it is an attempt to tease out (draw into the light, Conrad would say) a rationale, or counter-rationale, working both in and, perhaps, against literature's very canon. That the texts all come from the high-modernist period is no coincidence either—for isn't that when an exponentially accelerating industrialization, its accompanying technologies and ideologies, not only consolidated their claim (staked at least a century earlier) as the prime subject of literature and art but also radically reshaped its forms? Perhaps I'm hoping, in some paranoid (Pynchon-influenced) way, for a *Eureka!* instant; hoping to unearth a codex, a Rosetta Stone that would decode this moment and its legacy, both outside of and within—even *as*—literature. That, of course, is as much a fantasy as the Romantic/tragic one of owning one's own death: there is no single codex. But, I'd suggest, the closest thing we're going to get to one is the corpus of Mallarmé. Not only did he break form down until it reached its own zero-degree; he carried out this overhaul as part of an ongoing and active theorization of literature itself. As Derrida points out, whatever else Mallarmé seems to be describing, he is always also writing about the operation *of* writing, feeling his way around the contours of the book-to-come, the *livre* to which everything is destined to belong. I've argued elsewhere that without Mallarmé there would be no Joyce; and the same could be said of everyone from William Burroughs to John Cage. Barthes summed up twentieth-century literary activity by saying: "All we do is repeat Mallarmé— but if it's Mallarmé we repeat, we do right." How much more relevant, then, is the great thinker of the "virtual," of total legibility and omni-data, to the twenty-first?

A million things could be said about Mallarmé and the subject still be barely breached. But we are running out of room—so let's, by way of sketching out a much, much larger conversation to be had, home straight in on this fact: that Mallarmé is obsessed with the question of the pause, the interval, the recess. In a sketch from *Divagations* that seems to rehearse, to a *t*, Conrad's scene of interrupted labor, he presents workmen, "artisans of elementary tasks," taking a break from digging, lying around in such a manner as to "honourably reserve the dimension of the sacred in their existence by a work stoppage, an awaiting, a suicide." In an 1885 letter to Verlaine he writes:

> In the final analysis, I consider the contemporary era to be a kind of interregnum for the poet, who has nothing

to do with it: it is too fallen or too full of preparatory effervescence for him to do anything but keep working, with mystery, so that later, or never, and from time to time sending the living his calling card—some stanza or sonnet—so as not to be stoned by them if they knew he suspected that they didn't exist.

An extraordinary formulation: the poet, occupying the interregnum, is dead—by implication, since he's differentiated from "the living" to whom he sends his calling card (the work). But, in so doing, he refrains from giving the lie to the pretense of their existence—in other words, and at the risk of being not just once but twice dead (stoned, martyred), the poet plays the role of Addie Bundren. Plays it from the recess: another passage in *Divagations* pictures Villiers de L'Isle-Adam, his great tome forever kept from sight, withheld, reserved, knocking at the front door "like the sound of an hour missing from clock faces":

Midnights indifferently thrown aside for his wake, he who always stood beside himself, and annulled time as he talked: he waved it aside as one throws away used paper when it has served its function; and in the lack of ringing to sound a moment not marked on any clock, he appeared...

Yet this timeless appearance, "from the point of view of History," is not "untimely" but "punctual"—for, Mallarmé continues, "it is not contemporary with any epoch, not at all, that those who exalt all signification should appear"; they are both "projected several centuries ahead" and "turned toward the past." Both poetry and history demand such an appearance, *and* at the same time find themselves quite at a loss to locate it within their own parameters, their bounds or measures. In "L'action restreinte" this situation takes on a distinctly political hue. We are, Mallarmé tells us, as he sketches a Pynchonesque scenario of rapid transit though some great metropolis, approaching a tunnel, "the epoch," a "forever time":

> time unique in the world, since because of an event I have still to explain, there is no Present, no—a present does not exist... Lack the Crowd declares in itself, lack—of everything. Ill-informed anyone who would announce himself his own contemporary, deserting, usurping with equal impudence, when the past ceased and when a future is slow to come, or when both are mingled perplexedly to cover up the gap... So watch out and be there.

There is, in the offing, lurking, "pulsing in the unknown womb of the hour," an *event*—yet one that cannot name itself, nor even find a solid time-platform to arise and stand on. No wonder Alain Badiou turns to Mallarmé when he wants to elucidate his core or signature concept: the event, which, standing on the edge of the void so as to interpose itself between the void and itself (another doubling accretion), has "no acceptable ontological matrix." Calling up the "eternal circumstances" of the shipwreck in *Un Coup de Des*, Badiou calls Mallarmé "a thinker of the event-drama, in the double sense of the staging of its appearance-disappearance":

> every event, apart from being localized by its site, initiates the latter's ruin *with regard to the situation*, because it retroactively names its inner void. The "shipwreck" alone gives us the allusive debris from which (in the one of the site) the undecidable multiple of the event is composed.

Fine. But what would Mallarmé's un-named event *be*? Political revolution? Poetic epiphany? As Badiou points out, the central verb in *Un Coup de Des*, the one around which the whole text turns, is *hésite*: the master's dice-clasping hand, poised above the waves, holds back (like that of Blanchot's judge) from leaping into action, from descending to unleash the decisive cast. The only name that we could really give this "undecidable multiple" is Wait.

Derrida, too, turns at a key point in the trajectory of his thinking to Mallarmé—specifically, to the short text *Mimique* (which has been variously translated as "Dumb-show," "Mime," "Mimicry" and "Mimesis"). There, contemplating a mime-artist whose degree-zero corporeality renders his body both tool and subject of his performance, Mallarmé claims that what is illustrated is

> but the idea, not any actual action, in a Hymen (out of which flows Dream), tainted with vice yet sacred, between desire and fulfillment, penetration and remembrance; here anticipating, there recalling, in the future, in the past, *under the false appearance of a present*. That is how the mime operates, whose act is confined to a perpetual allusion without breaking the ice in the mirror: he thus sets up a medium, a pure medium, of fiction.

Derrida, of course, homes straight in on the *between*, hearing in Mallarmé's *entre* the *antra* of a cave or grotto, the *antara* of an interval. "What counts here," he writes, "is the *between*, the in-between-ness of the hymen"—symbol of marital union (Addie's and Anse's, for example) *and* membrane denoting separateness, through which "difference without presence appears, or rather baffles the process of appearing, by dislocating any orderly time at the center of the present." It is this baffling dislocation that sets up the "pure medium of fiction." *Fiction* would not be un-truth, as in Wait's lie or double-lie, or Addie's systematic pretense; nor would it be story, in Mann's sense of the unfolding of a narrative around temporal flow; rather, it would be recessionality itself. Fiction would be Hammertime.

Between. In *Un Coup de Des*, in the long pause initiated by the master's frozen gesture, a figure appears, feather—or pen—in cap: Hamlet, Western literature's most celebrated avatar of hesitation. Everyone and everything in that play is suspended: between order and execution, word and deed, heaven and hell. Even death is recessive: Hamlet wishes for its consummation but sees only continuity, the gerund—which, of course, gives him pause; Polonius's body starts to rot and smell under the staircase; the passage of Ophelia's into the ground is interrupted. Re-reading it recently, I was struck by the number of times *Julius Caesar* was knowingly alluded to within its pages (an unusual move for Shakespeare)—which, in turn, sent me back to Brutus's complaint about his own restless delay:

> Since Cassius first did whet me against Caesar,
> I have not slept.
> Between the acting of a dreadful thing
> And the first motion, all the interim is

> Like a phantasma, or a hideous dream:
> The Genius and the mortal instruments
> Are then in council; and the state of man,
> Like to a little kingdom, suffers then
> The nature of an insurrection.

Acting, here, means (once more) the precise opposite of action: it means the conception of the action to be done, and the foundation of the baffling interim that both conjoins this to and separates this from its consummation, its "first motion." *Like a phantasma, or a hideous dream.* Tool-downage, implements (*instruments*) idle, waiting. In this most political of plays, this recess is called *council*, and man's being a *state . . . a little kingdom*. Yet what's truly revolutionary (in all senses of the word) here is *not* the putative end-goal, the murder of the Emperor or overthrow of state; it is the interim itself. *Then* is the time where insurrection lurks: *then . . . then*—he says it twice, the temporal qualifier doubles or accretes, as though to open up and ground its referent: the interim, interim-time. And that, as we know, is the time of fiction.

2014

Blurring the Sublime
On Gerhard Richter

IN 2003, Gerhard Richter made four paintings with the same title: *Silicate*. Large oil-on-canvas pieces, these show latticed rows of light- and dark-gray blobs whose shapes quasi-repeat as they race across the frame, their angle modulating from painting to painting. When angled horizontally, they suggest strips of film bearing identical (or near identical) sequences but running at different speeds, all of them too fast for any image-content to be made out; when angled askew, they suggest out-of-focus close-ups of a bath-mat or worn carpet—or, perhaps, aerial views, similarly out of focus, of a gridded city.

In fact, what they're actually depicting is a photo, plucked from the *Frankfurter Allgemeine Zeitung*, of a computer-generated simulacrum of reflections from the silicon dioxide found in insects' shells. The compound is a prime ingredient of window-glass and fiber-optic cable; a semi-conductor, it's also a mainstay of computer chips. The article accompanying the source photo described research being conducted into structural colors—that is, colors that result from surface textures that refract, rather than contain, pigment. What seems, at first glance, an op art abstraction thus turns out, when unpacked, to contain an entire disquisition on the meshing of the "natural" world (insects) with its synthetic reproductions both inherent (shell-reflections) and exterior (scientific visual modeling); on the surfaces through which we look (windows) and vectors along which we relay or broadcast information (cables); on digital technology; and on color and its spectrum—which, of course, means both on painting and on light itself, the very ground and possibility of vision.

There's a tendency to discuss the art of the last hundred years in terms of binary oppositions: abstract versus figurative; conceptual versus craft-based; painting versus photography; and so on. The art of Gerhard Richter, who since the seventies has been almost universally acknowledged as a late-modern master, reduces these binaries to rubble. Here's a painter whose work is inseparable from photography; a man so devoted to craft that he reportedly makes his students construct their own palate-trolleys before allowing them to raise a brush in anger, yet who indulges in Beuys-style performances in which he lounges on a staircase grasping a wire (as in the 1968 piece *Cable Energy*), or Debordian critiques of consumer culture in which he installs himself on pedestal-mounted furniture amidst a soundscape of advertising slogans (as in the 1963 piece *Living with Pop: A Demonstration of Capitalist Realism*); who exhibits color-charts alongside pastoral landscapes; places mirrors around his paintings; photographs a single gray brushstroke from 128 different angles and lays these out in a large grid; or projects a yellow one, massively enlarged, onto fresh canvas and repaints it as a giant twenty-meter streak . . . I could go on and on: his versatility and scope are stunning.

Born in 1932 in Dresden, Richter studied at the city's Academy of Fine Art, then worked as a darkroom assistant and socialist-realist muralist before fleeing the DDR for Düsseldorf in 1961. Even before he left, he'd been exposed to such Western figures as the canvas-slashing Fontana and the paint-dribbling Pollock, and his earliest work betrays their influence. The piece that he himself presents as his first "proper" one, though, painted in 1962, depicts, in sober tones and utterly representational mode, a plain white table—or, rather, would depict this if it weren't for the large blur sitting at the picture's center. The unlikely combination is pure Richter: a preoccupation with the everyday and unadorned (a favorite expression of his, repeated in numerous correspondence, is *Es ist wie's ist*: "it is how it is"), married to a sense of some kinetic violence lurking either at the heart of these or at the interface between them and the viewer. Subsequent paintings—of toilet-roll holders, or of promotional pictures of new makes of car, or holidaying families posing for a snapshot, or statesmen blinking in the flashbulb glare of public scrutiny, or tribesmen doing the same before *National Geographic*'s gaze—would repeatedly involve some form of blurring: it quickly became Richter's trademark.

What is a blur? It's a corruption of an image, an assault upon its clarity, one that turns transparent lenses into opaque shower curtains, gauzy veils. Richter painted a lot of curtains; he had a curtain-painting hanging in his Düsseldorf studio, beside the curtain. He had, of course, left his own past behind an iron one; many of the blurred snapshot-scenes he produced in the sixties were of relatives he'd never see again, childhood locations become inaccessible. Beyond reflecting his own situation, the blur serves as a perfect general metaphor for memory, its degradation, for the Ozymandian corrosion wrought by time. One blurred Richter painting reproduces badly taken tourist snaps of Egypt, in which pyramids and temples lose their shapes and scale and grandeur. "I blur to make everything equal, everything equally important and equally unimportant," he explained.

Flashbulbs, snapshots, reportage: above all else, the blur recalls camera movement and errors of printing. The vast majority of Richter's paintings aren't directly "of" the thing they purport to show, but rather of magazine or photo-album reproductions of it. He'll often hammer this point home by including surrounding text: captions and advertising copy, scrapbook annotations—which, of course, blur too. What Richter is at pains to foreground is the fact of *mediation*, the presence, at the very origin and base of every piece, of technologies of mass production, of repetition. He not only overwrites our perceptual relation to the world by rerouting it through its glitch-ridden mediating screens; he also brings this logic to bear on the history of art. He remakes Vermeer's *Woman Reading at Window*, not only hazing it up but also, vitally, replacing the letter the original figure holds in her fingers—a unique, hand-written article with one addressee—with a newspaper: an impersonal, mass-produced media object. Blurring up Titian's *Annunciation*, he turns the image into what, for ninety-nine percent of its viewers, it already was: a reproduction of a reproduction, a third-generation bootleg.

That Richter homes in on the *Annunciation* is doubly significant, since Titian's masterpiece concerns itself with divine revelation, with the act of making known. Throughout Richter's oeuvre, a double-play is going on, a struggle being fought within each work between showing and hiding, with the result that each work performs a logic-defying feat of hiding-*in-the-act-of*-showing, of revealing hiddenness itself. In a recent interview with Nicholas Serota, Richter waxes all Heideggerean—or, in fact, Rumsfeldian—when Serota asks him: "Do you think painting is about discovering the unknown or the known?" The "known," he answers, "which we see and experience, which effects us and we have to react to...that is the most important thing"—but then, immediately *volte-fac*ing, he goes on to claim that when a subject "turns into the unknown, into what it was, that has an excitement all of its own." Painting, he concludes, has to retain "something incomprehensible." On occasion his own works have, despite their patina of opaque non-disclosure, divulged secrets of which even he was unaware. Two snapshot-derived paintings from 1965 and 1966, a nondescript image of the infant Richter with his aunt, and an equally generic childhood picture of his first wife and her family standing by a snowy road, seemed unconnected when he made them. But it transpired, years later, that the father-in-law posing in the second was a Nazi gynecologist who'd sterilized scores of mentally ill women in the same district in which the aunt in the first work, a schizophrenic, had herself been sterilized and euthanized in 1945. The subject of one painting had, at least by association and quite possibly literally, killed the subject of the other.

There's always violence lurking within Richter's images. When, in 1968, he painted aerial views of cities, the series was automatically framed by the bomber-planes he'd painted five years earlier. In *Townscape Paris*, buildings and monuments melt and implode in a series of streaks and smears. Is this paint smudging, or is he picturing the city being nuked? The ambiguity's deliberate: destruction is absorbed into the very act of representing; painting and bombing become one and the same gesture. No sooner had he finished this series than he turned his attention to mountain ranges, blasting their peaks to ruins through the formal modulations to which he subjected them. A later series, from 1975, is so blurred that it will strike most viewers as entirely abstract— until the two main words in all the works' titles, "tourist" and "lion," prompt them to squint and pick out the zoo visitor being ripped apart. Again, form and subject matter merge completely in the veiled divulgence of a ferocious primal scene: the paint becomes the lion, devouring figuration in a frenzy of power and movement. By the eighties Richter was dragging squeegees across paintings' surfaces, smearing (over the next two decades) everything from Venice to a forest to his third wife and newborn child in an astonishing annihilation of the difference between marking and erasing, revealing and obscuring, creating and destroying.

Richter's most famous series is *18th October 1977*. Painted eleven years after the events they address, the fifteen works—gray, small and undramatic—show members of the

Baader-Meinhof Group: a youthful picture; a post-capture mugshot; the record player in which a gun was smuggled into prison; a suicided prisoner; and so on. Derived from press and police photographs that Richter, naturally, has blurred, the images are remarkable for the dual pull they exert towards, on the one hand, monumentality and, on the other, monochrome monotony. In another recent interview, Richter uses the term *ansehnlich*, or "considerable," to describe the effect of rescuing an image from the endless rush of media and paying it the attention—the devotion, we could say—of crafting it into a unique work of art. The Baader-Meinhof paintings are *ansehnlich*, to be sure—but they're neither heroic nor condemnatory nor in any way resolved. "Their horror," Richter says, "is the horror of the hard-to-bear refusal to answer, to explain, to give an opinion." The pictures, ultra-loaded as they are, reject any attempt to bring their subject matter into focus along perspectival lines of ideology or pathos or transcendence. They represent, as Richter puts it, "a leave-taking from any specific doctrine of salvation." History is not there to be redeemed and held up in divine synthesis, least of all through art: rather, like a chair, or toilet-roll holder, or gramophone, *Es ist wie's ist.*

Since 1972, Richter has intermittently exhibited, under the title *Atlas*, the vast collection of source-images from which his work is drawn (he's also published it in book form with the same title). *Atlas*, perhaps, is Richter's greatest work, because it contains all the others. Flipping through it is like picking through the entrails—or, perhaps more fittingly, the source-code—of not only Richter's oeuvre but also the twentieth century and, perhaps, of Western art in its entirety. Here are bombs, fridges, hard-core porn, the surface of the moon; here's a cruise ship, an electric light, a waterfall, a diver frozen in mid-somersault, the image over-gridded; here's a warship, a suburban street, stags on a mountain, heaps of bodies in an Auschwitz yard. Here are the Baader-Meinhof photos; here's that hapless tourist with his lion; here's one of Richter's own doodles. The pictures are ordered by their formal qualities—color-gradations, shapes and angles—rather than thematically, which sets up a visual taxonomy in which all subjects are both reduced to equal terms *and* augmented by their juxtaposition with the others. He intervenes in many of the images, sticking lines of tape on urban sprawls to identify their axes, or extrapolating the pattern of a tower block's stacked-up balconies, repeating this in the next image as pure abstract geometry, then morphing it back into a sketch of plinths for an imaginary exhibition of his work. It's as though, like some symbolic safe-cracker, he were running through all possible combinations and all modulations of the world's image-bank; or,

like some ancient Gnostic monk or rabbi, reeling the mutating names of God off in an incantatory votive list with
neither origin nor end—the vital difference being that Richter's universe is godless. This, perversely, makes it all the
more revelatory. It's revelatory in the sense that the philos-
opher Giorgio Agamben uses the term: profane without
redemption, just irreparably *thus*.

When, in 2007, the atheist Richter was commissioned to
design a stained-glass window for Cologne's cathedral, he
had colored squares installed in electronically generated random configurations, parts of which he then repeated across
the 113-square-meter space—again, extrapolating patterns,
taxonomizing the forms and sequences chance throws out.
The work caused a furore, with a cardinal complaining (using, albeit inadvertently, delightfully apt language) that the
work doesn't "clearly reflect our faith." Too right it doesn't.
From an art perspective, though, what's more important
than Richter's rejection of the divine is his parallel rebuffal
of the sublime. Like virtually all German artists of his generation, Richter at times conducts a dialogue with Roman-
ticism. But road signs replace church spires in his landscapes;
waves and clouds are fragmented, isolated, collaged and
inverted; icebergs are laid out in multiplying rows, like in
school geography textbooks. The fascination is retained—
but it's a fascination voided of sublimity, wedded instead to

repetition, reproduction, an interrogation of the act of looking and the technologies through which this act takes place.

Here, as everywhere in Richter's work, the gaze—of the
artist, of the viewer, of the whole optical field—has been
purged of the pathetic fallacy, of sentimentality, of ideologies
of "naturalness." This is what sets him head and shoulders
above his contemporaries Beuys and Kiefer—who, for all
their brilliance, fall into the trap of uncritically reiterating
the Romantic aesthetic that segued so seamlessly, with its
dual fetishes of blood and earth, its sentimentalizing of history, into Nazism and finds its contemporary expression in
vague cultural notions of authenticity and "spirituality." To
make the leap beyond such consoling and reactionary ba-
nalities—and to do this without getting snared in that other
trap, the one so much of Britart made its home in, namely
irony—that is the aesthetic challenge of our era.

I'll end, given the timing of this essay, with a series of
paintings Richter made in 2005. Titled simply *September*,
and numbered "series No. 911" in his internal cataloguing
system, they grew from a notebook drawing—an extrapo-
lated mutation of who knows how many other mutated
images—that Richter himself considered abstract until his
friend Benjamin Buchloh looked at it and said: "Oh, that's
the World Trade Center being attacked." So, like the tourist
finding his figure even as he lost it to the paint-lion's swirling

carnage, the twin towers loom into view, in the completed series, out of shockingly gorgeous light-blue backgrounds, before disappearing, at each painting's top, in clouds of billowing gray, while small metallic streaks—denoting planes, or media, or violence, or perhaps just paint—blur as they hurtle across the canvas.

2011

The Prosthetic Imagination of David Lynch

THERE'S AN EARLY David Lynch film called *The Amputee*. Two films, in fact: he made it twice, with the same script, same shots, same everything. Explaining the duplication years later, he tells his interviewer that the American Film Foundation wanted to test two types of video stock, so he used the opportunity to produce a short, recording it on both types for comparison. He did this not without misgivings: that the American *Film* Foundation should be consorting with a format that might turn out to be film's nemesis "gave me a sadness." In the film itself, a woman with two stumps instead of legs is seen writing a letter, while an audio voiceover renders the content of this silent process. The content itself is pretty conventional, involving some interpersonal psychological entanglement or other. But this is relegated to the background: the film's prime action, what we actually *see*, is a nurse dressing the stumps: unraveling bandages, pumping liquid over mounds of misformed scar-tissue, letting it drain and dribble out of cavities and craters. Pure Lynch already: a ghoulish fascination with traumatized flesh and its contortions, set against a backdrop of anxiety about the medium, the very material, in which the drama is being rendered.

Try to count the instances of deformity in Lynch's work—of dwarves, cripples and characters missing arms and legs—or of people *being* deformed on camera (having their limbs chopped off, blown off or carried off by dogs), and you'll lose count pretty quickly. To interpret Lynch's repeated featuring of disability as a liberal, "equal-opportunity" type gesture would be wildly wide of the mark; yet seeing it as a kind of shorthand for moral perversity, like Richard III's hunched back in Shakespeare's play, would be just as wide. Deformity, for Lynch, is not simply thematic: it is, we could say, only slightly punning, *instrumental*. What the continual, almost systematic replacement in his films of body parts and faculties by instruments—by crutches, wheelchairs, hearing aids and ever-weirder apparatuses sometimes as large as rooms—produces is a whole prosthetic order, a world of which prosthesis is not just a feature but a fundamental term, an ontological condition. And the implications of this world, this order, are, as Lynch himself might put it, big.

FOR FREUD, prosthesis is the essence of technology. "With all his tools," he writes in *Civilization and its Discontents*, "man improves his own organs, both motor and sensory, or clears away the barriers to their functioning." Ships, airplanes, telescopes and cameras, gramophones and telephones—all these afford man the omnipotence and omniscience he attributes to his gods, thus making him *"eine Art Prosthesengott"*: a kind of god with artificial limbs, a prosthetic god. "When he puts on all his auxiliary organs he is truly magnificent," Freud writes; "but" (he continues) "those organs have not grown on to him and they still give him much trouble at times." Man's technological appendages both enhance and diminish him. It's what Hal Foster, in his book *Prosthetic Gods*, calls "the double logic of the prosthesis": an addition that threatens, or marks, a subtraction.

This double logic is writ large in Lynch's films. That Geoffrey's father in *Blue Velvet* is strapped up, astronaut-like, to apparati of the highest order is due not to some heroic cosmic voyaging but rather to his having been struck down by a heart attack, immobilized, made pathetic; meeting Geoffrey's gaze with his, all he can do is cry. As Geoffrey returns from visiting him in hospital this same logic is expanded to provide the film's inciting incident: his discovery, among waste ground, of a severed ear heralds the onset of a world of amplified, recorded and transmitted sound, where Dorothy Vallens sings into trademark Lynchean microphones, Frank Booth and his entourage mime to tape cassettes, and crackling walkie-talkies hold the key to life and death. This world is both exhilarating and threatening. And its onset actually came much sooner in Lynch's oeuvre than Geoffrey's discovery of the severed natural organ it replaces: from the opening seconds of *Eraserhead* we're immersed in what sounds like a mixture of loudspeaker static and industrial noise, a neo-Rilkean *Gerausch* that represents nothing but sheer, mechanical technology, reified and roaring. Off in a signal-box somewhere, a sweaty, tar-coated figure yanks a lever and a homunculus-like thought-conception slips out of Henry's brain. His biological and mental life already outsourced to machines, Henry ends the film *becoming* one himself, his head fed through a pencil-shaping press whose cogs and belts and punchers move with an automated regularity that's suggestive of the action of a Steenbeck editing machine or cinema projector. If we bear in mind that the young, broke Lynch, like the pen- and pencil-carrying Henry prior to being laid off, held down a day job as a printer, and has professed through his career an admiration for the writer (and clerical pencil pusher) Kafka, whose presence haunts *Eraserhead*, then it almost seems as though what we're witnessing is literature's own extension, its simultaneous dismemberment and augmentation, into the medium of cinema, which serves as its prosthesis. But that's by the by: what's certain is that Henry is transformed, and that his transformation is not only physical but metaphysical as well. The shavings of his brain become glittering constellations, like Greek heroes turning into gods, and an angelic singer lurking in the radiator (which itself is panned to from the gramophone: the metaphysics, for Lynch, always lie in the machine) sings to him of heaven. It's an exaltation—and its opposite, a complete abjection: the angel is disgusting, grossly deformed, and Henry, trapped in the hellhole of his flat, has killed his son, gone mad and been tried, condemned and decapitated.

Technology, as our prosthesis, makes us godlike and less-than-human in one and the same move: that we know. But it gets more complex: technology, in Lynch's work, is *itself* degraded. The machinery surrounding Henry isn't the streamlined gadgetry of a future techno-utopia but rather the decaying and run-down relics of an exhausted industrial past: barely functioning lifts whose cables feebly whirr, old pipes and half-dead factories whose steam wheezes as sickly as the lungs of his diseased child. At play is not just a double logic but a double-double logic, in which the realm of the technological is as two-sided as the mankind it pushes and pulls in two directions. The bare-topped, tar-coated god who pulls the levers that control Henry's destiny is, like the disfigured angel-lady, disease-ridden, with plague-like boils across his face and chest. Nonetheless, the relationship between him and Henry is one of operator-operated.

HERE WE COME ACROSS another way to think about prosthesis: as a form of puppetry. In his 1810 story-cum-essay "On the Marionette Theatre," the German Romantic writer Heinrich von Kleist recounts a meeting, in a fairground, with a choreographer who, watching marionettes being manipulated, marvels at the way in which dance "could be entirely transferred to the realm of mechanical forces" and "controlled by a crank." "Have you heard," the choreographer asks the narrator, "of the artificial legs designed by English craftsmen for those unfortunates who have lost their limbs?" The implication is clear: prosthetic-clad man is like a puppet—which begs the question: who's the puppeteer?

This question is a central one for Lynch. His films abound in instances of control, in scenes in which control itself is dramatized. "I can make him do anything I please!" Frank boasts to brothel owner Ben of his captive Geoffrey; his other captive, Dorothy, he manipulates night after night, telling her "Sit down!"; "Open your legs!"; "Don't look at me!" Dorothy then does the same to Geoffrey, holding a knife to his throat and hissing at him "Undress!" or, later, "Hit me!"—both of which he does. *The Elephant Man*, which, like Kleist's text, opens in a nineteenth-century fairground in which puppets are displayed, sees John Merrick being alternately bullied into standing up and turning round to order for the paying carny public and more kindly but no less decisively prompted to perform the same maneuvers by his doctor, who then teaches him to speak and tells him what to say.

Telling people what to say, how to move their body or where to direct their gaze is, of course, part and parcel of making films, and, to a degree, we have to recognize in all these instances of control a kind of *mise-en-abîme* of Lynch's own role as a director. But there's a metaphysical dimension to it too. For Kleist, puppetry lays bare a complex process through which man, robbed of the pure, naive grace of a puppet by self-consciousness, might regain it by advancing so far into knowledge that he re-emerges on the other side to "appear most pure in that human form which either has no consciousness at all or possesses infinite consciousness— that is, either in a marionette or in a god"—an event, the choreographer informs the narrator, that would constitute "the last chapter in the history of the world." Think of the network of control in *Wild at Heart*: it also has a metaphysical dimension: divine and supernatural forces, voodoo priestesses and witches. As Marianna makes a call to Santos, who calls the shamanic-sounding Mr. Reindeer, who calls calliper-clad Grace Zabriskie, who calls Bobby Peru, all of them exchanging phrases of an incantatory character, like spells, she watches Sailor and Lulu's progress in her glass ball, as though she were Athena gazing down on Odysseus's troubled journey home. As Lulu becomes all too aware as she watches the Wicked Witch ride along beside their car, mortals are mingling with gods, not all of them good ones. In describing Bobby Peru as "a dark angel," she's not simply using figurative speech: called down upon them from the elevated realm that arches over terrestrial space like a tele-fiber-theo-optic mesh, he is one.

Wild at Heart's main template, which, alongside its apocalyptic images of ozone-depleted heat-death and mass automobile carnage, it keeps self-consciously invoking, is the ultimate cinematic fable of divinity and puppetry: *The Wizard of Oz*, in which the god who controls everything and can make all things happen turns out, at the end of the technicolor rainbow, to be no more than a feeble man cranking a crappy, low-tech, carny-type contraption. Incredibly, mainstream, commercial cinema managed to enact in 1939 the subversive fantasy that William Burroughs would spend decades toiling in the underground and avant-garde to for-mulate: the fantasy that the Control Room or Reality Studio that maintains the illusion that in turn conserves repressive order can be revealed for what it is, rumbled and blown open. For Burroughs, this day, when it arrives, will not only prompt panicked cries that "the director is on set," but also herald the end of the film—that is, perhaps, the end of time, and, certainly, the death of God (who, after all, is no more than a hack director, a degenerate crank-operator whose power over us makes "ventriloquist dummies" of us). Here, again, we come back to prosthesis: for Burroughs, God is like an irksome and unnecessary limb or organ. Learning of a tribe whose small toes (quite unnecessary for stability) are genetically programed to self-amputate in adolescence, he pictures God, too, withering and dropping off. "He atro-phied and fell off me like horrible old gills," he has a putative "survivor" of this miracle (or counter-miracle) confide to a journalist, "And I feel ever so much better."

WITH ALL THIS IN MIND, then, I want to look, quickly, at the triumvirate of what, if Lynch receives his full critical due in future years, will probably come to be referred to, *á la* Shakespeare, as his "problem films": the ones that, lacking a stable reality field, are fraught with ontological discrepancies.

The first of these, *Lost Highway*, is an orgy of deformity and bodily shut-down. Fred doesn't simply murder Renee, he dismembers her; Richard Prior makes a final film appearance, all decrepit in his wheelchair; there's the dwarfish Mystery Man with his telephone, another big prosthetic ear (in the course of inventing the telephone, Alexander Bell stole a corpse's ear so he could mechanically reproduce its inner workings; both his mother and his wife were deaf). The Mystery Man, with his illuminated face, is also a kind of angel: here, too, humans mix with gods—and do so through a technologically-enabled interface of videos and sound equipment, fine-tuned (and not so fine-tuned) car engines and wireless sets. If *Eraserhead*'s mechanics are run down, *Lost Highway*'s supernatural realm of technology is blighted too, glitch-ridden: burglar alarms disabled, tapes peppered with white noise, radios prone to interference from the other channel.

What's this film *about*? The same as all of Lynch's films: the outsourcing of the self and of reality to their prostheses—and the outsourcing of what is at once the triumph and catastrophe of God's death to the prosthetic realm as well. God dies in *Lost Highway*, make no mistake: Dick

Laurent—note the initials: DL—the one who makes the porno movies running on a loop in the control room of desire, is butchered gruesomely in front of the Mystery Man's camera; as he dies, he half-quotes Burroughs's refrain about his prime God-stand-in, The Ugly American, telling Fred: "You and me Mister: we can really out-ugly them sum-bitches, can't we?" Time, at this point, reaches the end of its reel, comes full circle, and the film ends with the same, Nietzschean announcement it began with: "Dick Laurent is dead." Slavoj Žižek, pondering this line, sees it as a carrier of a psychoanalytic Real that circularly reasserts itself through the repetition of a moment in the linguistic chain, a phrase. But it's not just a phrase: it's a phrase spoken *through the intercom*—yet another electronic ear that extends its owner's reach beyond the borders of his house but also leaves him open to infection, to unwittingly inviting strangers in. I'm tempted to say that the film, ultimately, is *about* the intercom itself. *Talk, Listen, Door*—the three terms written above its buttons—contain the sum of all its moves. But the prosthetic ear will have to share star billing with the big prosthetic eye—which makes the Mystery Man the "realest," most objective character in the whole film, by virtue of the fact that it is he who holds this eye: he is quite simply, like the star of Dziga Vertov's landmark film of the same name, the Man with the Movie Camera.

The same state of affairs persists in *Mulholland Drive*. People who try to work out what's "really" going on in it are wasting their time, since the whole drama of the film is that of a reality-field trying to hold itself together after its sovereign guarantor (in this case, not an over-virile father figure but rather the female object of an obsessive lesbian love) has been assassinated. It tries (and fails, and tries again) to do this through the medium of film—the narratives, scripts, and personae of Hollywood. Only the reel is real. The man in the Control Room this time—Mr. Roke—is almost pure prosthesis, his already tiny, crippled body dwarfed yet further by the spacious, hi-tech chamber from which, via intercom again, he calls the shots. In an astonishing scene involving human puppetry, the heroines attend a cabaret that's all mechanics, with the singer miming to a pre-recorded tape. What's astonishing about the scene is not that the artifice is unmasked (indeed, it's even announced by the compère at the show's outset), but rather the inversion that takes place: as the tape plays, Betty shakes, literally "moved" by it; then, as the singer mouths along to the words *estoy llorando*, "I am crying," she and Rita cry! Technology is no longer an appendage to the human; rather, humans have become technology's prosthesis.

By *Inland Empire*, it's no longer even tiny humans occupying the central chamber but, rather, mechanical rabbits, moving robotically to canned laughter. In the Control Room, the marionettes: the puppets operate us. Opening with a close-up shot of speeding gramophone grooves overlaid with the crackling announcement of a radio play, then cutting straight to CCTV images of people with blanked-out faces, then to a woman watching television—four media profiled in less than as many minutes—the film announces at its outset that its subject will be mediation itself. What follows is all glitch, all interference, slippage between one reality-field and another as lines, situations and identities morph into and out of one another, quasi-repeating. "There's a vast network," says Freddy, "an ocean of possibilities." It's this network that "Nikki" navigates, encountering an architecture that, I'd suggest, can best be understood as "digital"— digital in the strict computing sense of information storage, relay and configuration. Like a gamer, she must find her way towards the inner chamber, negotiating levels that regress and embed each other; like a hacker, she must crack its source code, break the game's own system, bring it crashing down. To put it in Kleistian terms, she must come to the point where no consciousness and infinite consciousness coincide, gods and marionettes become one, the world's last chapter. Not only is this logic digital; the medium in which it takes place, the very matter on which Lynch shot it, is as well. What's been amputated, cut, removed from this film is the film itself, replaced not (as in *The Amputee*) by video but by virtual technology, the ones and zeros of computer code.

The world's last chapter; cinema's prosthesis. This, perhaps, is what we're witnessing at *Inland Empire*'s end. Against the agonized apocalyptic ecstasy of Nina Simone's "Sinnerman," a song that tells of what happens at time's end, "all on them day," a girl who, with a gear stick for a leg, embodies all the amputees and car-crash victims, all the dwarves, puppets and freaks in Lynch's oeuvre, hobbles onto a stage on which all the film's players, revels ended now, are gathered—and, surveying the scene with a smile, murmurs: "Sweet."

2009

From Feedback to Reflux
Kafka's Cybernetics of Revolt

LETTER TO HIS FATHER (the "original" title, the one Max Brod baptized the text with after Kafka's death, is *Brief an den*—the, not *seinen*, his—*Vater*) was written in 1919. Reading it almost a century later, what most jumps out at me from the opening salvos is an image, a micro-conceit. Explaining to his father that the problem isn't simply that their relationship has lost its way but that, on top of this, the responsibility for this errancy is laid *by* his father entirely at *his*, Franz's, feet, Kafka sardonically quips: "as though I might have been able, with something like a touch on the steering-wheel, to make everything quite different" (*als hätte ich etwa mit einer Steuerdrehung das Ganze anders einrichten können*). This is not the only time Kafka invokes this figure. An undated one-page story titled "The Helmsman" (*Der Steuermann*) presents a dream-like scenario in which the narrator, "standing at the helm in the dark night," is pushed aside by "a tall, dark man" and reduced to feebly and for-lornly crying: "Am I not the helmsman?"—then, less certainly, "Am I the helmsman ... ?"

What seems almost uncanny now is that Kafka's deployment of a specific nautical-navigational syntax anticipates by several decades the one that Norbert Wiener would carry out when naming his new form, or mode, of systems thinking. The term *cybernetics*, Wiener explains to readers in his 1950 book *Human Use of Human Beings: Cybernetics and Society*, is derived from *kubernetes*, Greek for "steersman" or "governor"—the latter of which, by Wiener's time, denotes not just the political position but also the inbuilt, self-regulatory device that allows steam engines to assess and respond to their own temperature-data, thus preventing breakdown through overheating. Beneath the banner of the term, Wiener elaborates a giant, almost universally applicable vision through which everything from economics to biology, psychology to media or law, can be both mapped and manipulated by being understood as an *information* or *communication* system—understood, that is, as a networked mechanism formed of and driven by a set of circuits, relays and, most importantly, feedback loops. Wiener's vision, its implicit logic, became the core one of the age of information, not to mention digital surveillance, that emerged throughout the late twentieth century and has established itself so forcefully at the outset of the twenty-first. And Kafka, it seems, shared it. We've long known that his work anticipates the Nazi terror, Stalinist bureaucracy and corporate capitalism that came in its wake; but it is becoming increasingly clear that it also adumbrates, both in spirit and to the very letter, and even when he seems to be talking about something else entirely, the unsettling world of Google and the NSA in which we live today.

No other writer, even after Wiener's coinage, let alone before it, has presented a more fundamentally cybernetic aesthetic than Kafka. Think of the hotel in *Amerika*, which functions (like Karl's uncle's desk with its moving panels and its "regulator" dial) as a giant information-relay device, with messenger boys carrying data held in back-up ledgers to and from back-room telephonists who harvest, transcribe, and despatch more data down their lines, while under-porters answer questions nonstop in the lobby. Or the labyrinthine secretariat of *The Castle*, in which one department forwards documents on to another while a "Control Authority" is set in place to iron out (supposedly) errors—a set-up that results in the message that K. originated being recited back to him. Or, of course, the gargantuan judicial infrastructure of *The Trial*, where letters, telegrams, phone calls and endless dossiers tail-chase each other in eternal circles. *Letter to His Father* is no less infused with this aesthetic than the novels are. An address *to* the father begins, in its very first sentence, by fielding an inquiry *from* the recipient as to why the sender has asserted a fear *of* the recipient—one feedback-loop embedding a second which, in turn, embeds a third. It draws to a close by envisioning an answer *to* the answer in which the letter's addressee, now speaking back, summarizes (and counteracts) the sender's complaints about himself—a similarly regressive circuitry—and signs off by hoping for a "correction that results from this rejoinder." Halfway through, the entire paternal-filial relationship is rendered as an algorithmic action/reaction formula: A gives B a piece of advice; the advice is rather toxic, and requires of B a damage-repairing exercise should B accept it; B is not obliged to accept it; if he does, it should not cause his whole future world to tumble down upon him. "And yet," Kafka concludes, "something of this kind does happen, but only for the very reason that A is you and B is myself."

There's the rub. Whereas Wiener's feedback loops are *corrective* ones, Kafka's, despite the ameliorating credo to which he half-heartedly pays lip service from time to time (and even then he can't refrain, when claiming that his letter will make both son's and father's living easier, from adding "and our dying"), have quite the opposite effect. They are, we could say, "fuckuptive." His father's response or countermove to any and every statement or proposition Kafka might put before him is negative, not only after the fact but even before it ("you have a dislike in advance of every one of my activities and particularly of the nature of my interest")—so much so that Kafka internalizes the response pattern and sabotages his own projects and aspirations preemptively. A self-defeating logic installs itself at the heart of all his putative moves, not least that of leaving the whole loop behind by, for example, marrying (an act, he reasons, that might finally propel him out of his father's orbit into "self-liberation and independence"): that would be akin to a prisoner escaping from prison *and* (since marriage reinstates the family structure) rebuilding the prison as a pleasure-seat for himself—an impossibility, since "if he escapes, he cannot do any rebuilding, and if he rebuilds, he cannot escape." To put it another way: the circuitry or system-architecture here is configured in such a way as to render unworkable any operation that the user (Kafka) might actually want to use it to perform; it induces serial and ineluctable instances of system-failure—while *itself* (as a bigger, overarching system whose goal is precisely to induce such instances of failure) functioning perfectly.

This is, to say the least, a paradoxical situation—one whose nature Kafka understands all too well. He knows, and frequently restates, that both he and his father are caught up in larger networks, larger meshes. Even as he reproaches him, he acknowledges that "you are entirely blameless"; he speaks of "our helplessness, yours and mine"; and of how he and his sisters discuss the "terrible trial that is pending between us and you... a trial in which ... you are a party too, just as weak and deluded as we are." The choice of metaphor is hardly accidental. Kafka had already written *The Trial* when he penned this letter; he even quotes from it. The same fuckuptive logic pervades that novel, a sense of being held within "a great organization" whose own buildings are nonetheless dilapidated, whose own functionaries are corrupt and incompetent and whose administrative procedures, even when adhered to, are inherently flawed, ensuring that pleas get filed in the wrong place, or lost, or simply never read. "Yet that, too," Advocate Huld informs Josef K., "was intentional." Same in *The Castle*: K. is held in limbo by a set of glitches and miscalculations given rise to by the very protocol set up between Departments A and B (that algorithmic shorthand again) to move things forward, prevented from carrying out his work as a land surveyor by the very letter that commends him for the land-surveying work he is supposedly already undertaking. And that's the point: the whole thing works because things don't quite work. The task, for both K.s, is not to navigate the alarmingly well-calibrated nodes and junctures of a streamlined mechanism, but rather to negotiate a set of errors, incompatibilities.

So is it for the third K., author-protagonist of *Letter*. Right at the outset, after skimming over a typical instance of counterproductive circularity (the general truth of my fear of you makes it impossible for me to utter any particular truth-statement about it), Kafka flags up incompatibilities between, first, thinking and speaking, then, speaking and writing. As versions of a larger system, language, these modes should be capable of running together, of passing content between one another (thus allowing him to articulate and set down his thoughts)—yet they can't. It's tempting for me, as a writer who believes in a kind of primacy of writing, writing about another writer with compatible beliefs, to claim that, for Kafka, the act of writing serves as a fortress against the overwhelming oppressiveness of social or familial life. And, certainly, Kafka is tempted to make this claim too: he notes down some of his father's meanest utterances, to store as later weaponry, and even, when alluding to his own books, states that "in writing and what is connected with it I have made some attempts at independence, attempts at escape." But he immediately acknowledges that he has done so only "with the very smallest of success; they will scarcely lead any further." Ultimately, Kafka is too clever for a naive belief that writing furnishes some heroic, self-affirming path to overcoming adversity. Writing, he admits to his father from the get-go, is no less a broken vehicle for conveying the message he is charged with. It, too, is rendered dysfunctional—partly by the lethal feedbacks and incompatibilities alluded to already, but, above and beyond these, by the fact that "[anyway] the magnitude of the subject goes far beyond the scope of my memory and power of reasoning." Rather than *Sache* (which he'll use one paragraph later), he chooses the word *Stoff* for "subject" here (*weil die Größe des Stoffs über mein Gedächtnis und meinen Verstand weit hinausgeht*): "stuff"—or, more viscerally, matter, inner substance. What the language- or communication-system, glitch-ridden though it may be in the first place, *ultimately* runs aground on isn't so much internal error as the sandbank of a vast material excess. If memory and power of reasoning were vessels, this gross stuff would spill and ooze from them; if they were membranes, it would rupture them, disgorge itself; it would then swell yet further, filling the surrounding space, and stay there, long outliving (to return to Kafka's own *Trial*-quote) its now-defunct carriers—dark, disgusting and, above all, shameful.

GILLES DELEUZE and Félix Guattari, in their brilliant short book *Kafka: Toward a Minor Literature*, decry the tendency of critics to treat guilt as the theological mainstay of their Kafka readings—that is, to see guilt as the abstract (and absolute) manifestation of a conventionally Judeo-Christian framework within which the works take place. Which doesn't mean guilt isn't vital to the works. To understand the role it plays, though, we should—once again—turn to the original. The German word for "guilt" is *Schuld*, which also means "debt." The double-sense of the term is far from lost on Chief Financial Officer Josef K., who treats his trial as a reckoning or book-balancing exercise—"no more than a business deal such as he had often concluded to the advantage of the Bank." Nor is it lost on *Letter*'s narrator, who has conducted his entire life "like a business man"—albeit one "who lives...without keeping any proper books...He makes a few small profits, which as a consequence of their rarity he keeps on pampering and exaggerating in his imagination, and for the rest only daily losses. Everything is entered, but never balanced." When the time comes for "drawing a balance," the audit concludes that "it is as though there had never been even the smallest profit, everything one single great liability [*Schuld*]."

Kafka's relation to his father is essentially an economic one, since, for him, economics form the grid onto which all other fields, not least that of identity itself, are plotted. "I have inherited a great deal from you and taken much too good care of my inheritance," he muses wrily when pondering his father's severity: one's "character" is no more than an economic measure; algorithmically, it could be rendered as *inherited sum* x *multiplied (or divided) by capital-management skills* y. His father has "magnificent commercial talents"; he was, through Kafka's childhood, "tied to the [family] business," so much so that "the business and you became one for me." Kafka, by contrast, shows no economic savvy; he has "never taken any interest in the business." Where his father has worked hard to accumulate wealth, the non-profit-generating Kafka, who recognizes "that it would have been possible for me really to enjoy the fruits of your great and successful work, that I could have turned them to account and continued to work with them," has been able to "enjoy what you gave, but only in humiliation, weariness, weakness, and with a sense of guilt [*Schuldbewußtsein*]. That was why I could be grateful to you for everything only as a beggar is." The son whose "valuation of myself was much more dependent on you than on anything else" bears his very existence "as an undeserved gift from you." As the anthropologist Marcel Mauss points out, a gift *obliges* its receiver, places him in debt. This is the debt that Kafka, tasked with "ingratitude," feels, at all turns and all times, as guilt. "I was penetrated by a sense of guilt"; "the child's exclusive sense of guilt"; "a boundless sense of guilt"; "fear and a sense of guilt"—the word crops up so many times I gave up trying to count it. The translators try to disperse it, modifying it into "shame" or "blame"; at one point they supply the sequence: "here again what accumulated was only a huge sense of guilt. On every side I was to blame. I was in debt to you." But where they vary, Kafka repeats—and where they separate "blame" and "debt" out into two closing sentences, Kafka needs only one because *his* thinking brooks no separation: "*Überdies sammelte sich ... wieder nur eine großes Schuldbewußtein an. Von allen Seiten her kam ich in Deine Schuld.*"

"Economics" is derived from the Greek *oikos*, which means "home" or "hearth"—the idea being that the economic realm allows an individual, a (male) head-of-household, to expand the dominion of his home-management beyond the bounds of his immediate property, thus enlarging the area over which he might exert control. Whether knowingly or not, *Letter* seems to follow this etymology with utter precision. Kafka's father lords it over his household; possessed of "a will to life, business, and conquest," he extends his domain out into the world through his commercial ventures (notice the slippage, as with the case of Irma for example, between children and employees: both are treated the same, since both form part of the same credit-and-debt empire). If man, at base, is *homo economicus*, if establishing and growing one's home and its domain is the "very great and very honourable"

trajectory one's life should follow, "the utmost a human being can succeed in doing at all," then Kafka's father's life has
followed that trajectory without deviation: not coming from
wealth himself, *he* got to found and multiply his *oikos*. The
children, by contrast, being born into *his* comfort, were denied that plot-line: "we were too well off…What you had
to fight for we received from your hand." What this means
territorially is that there is no unoccupied space left for them
to either found *in* or multiply *into*. "Sometimes," writes
Kafka, "I imagine the map of the world spread out flat and
you stretched out diagonally across it. And what I feel then
is that only those territories come into question for my life
that either are not covered by you or are not within your
reach. And, in keeping with the conception that I have of
your magnitude, these are not many and not very comforting
territories…"

There is no question, here, of sharing markets: for Kafka,
economics is a zero-sum game. Were the son to marry and
found his own hearth (and Kafka is crystal clear that "the
fundamental idea of both attempts at marriage was…to set
up house, to become independent"), this would diminish
the father's in direct proportion, oust him from his territory;
even a meek announcement by the former of a half-intent
to do so damages the latter's "sense of self-importance," spurring him to plan his emigration. Self-sufficiency, "breaking

away from home," was "not what you wanted at all, that you termed ingratitude, extravagance, disobedience, treachery, madness." Ottla's "escapade," her mini-breakout (she leaves the household and attempts to set up as a farm manager), causes the father blind, impotent fury; and besides, it is—predictably—short-lived, bankrupting itself quickly.

Kafka himself, for reasons we've already understood, doesn't even carry through his own mooted break-out efforts. Faced with his father's near-global monopoly, he does nonetheless come up with an economic strategy—one that could best be characterized by the term *withholding*. In another passage that deploys a bookkeeping and liability analogy, he describes his childhood sense of fraudulence—or, more precisely, of defrauding both his teachers and the world in general by advancing from grade to grade despite lacking any worth or merit: "Lessons," he writes, "and not only lessons but everything round about me, at that decisive age, interested me pretty much as a defaulting bank clerk, still holding his job and trembling at the thought of discovery, is interested in the small current business of the bank, which he still has to deal with as a clerk." It's a very telling conceit: the embezzling clerk does, after all, construct a kind of shadow economic territory of his own—not outside or independent of the bank for which he works, but rather in a negative or hidden zone within this; he amasses a perverse profit from the guilty debit of the sum withheld. This is Kafka's lot: any life capital he has amassed is precisely equivalent to that sum. If he has amassed knowledge, it is (he states, summarizing his father's argument) because "I have always dodged you and hidden from you, in my room, among my books." If he has amassed or clawed back any breathing space at all, it is because "I...cringed away from you, hid from you..." This motif—of furtive and systematic withholding, of "secretion"—crops up time and again.

Cringed. It's what insects do when you poke them: they withdraw, with a repulsive quiver, to the shadows. Kafka's withholding may form part of an elaborate psycho-economic strategy; but it takes place at a simple bodily level too. Here the base material side of things comes into play again: that gross stuff or stuffing, shamefully protruding. Throughout *Letter*, Kafka presents his own body as (depending on how you count it) both guilty excess *and* withheld debit. As an adolescent, he claims, "I shot up, tall and lanky, without knowing what to do with my lankiness." Corporeality is something that is awkward, *de trop*, and cries out for a hiding place. This impulse is mirrored in the bathing-hut anecdote: here, although the child's frame as he changes next to his strong-bodied father is small rather than large ("skinny, weakly, slight...a miserable specimen"), the sense of shame its mere physical presence gives rise to is the same: "What made me feel best was when you sometimes undressed first and I was able to stay behind in the hut alone and put off the disgrace of showing myself in public until at length you came to see what I was doing and drove me out of the hut." This scene is itself doubled in the *pavlatche* episode, in which Kafka the small child whimpering in his bed is dragged out by his father to the apartment building's semi-public courtyard-balcony (*pavlatche*), which gives rise to a lifelong (and, for a Prague Jew, ominously prescient) terror that some "huge man" or "ultimate authority" will come and pull him from his hiding place once more.

The tendency of Kafka in these scenes—the urge to stash, "embezzle" his own body from the public realm, dominion of his father—is core to his entire formation; and the prominence, or central role, allotted to his body here provides a material, corporeal base or underpinning to all the other scenes and aspects of his withholding. When "I rushed away from you," it was "in order to lie down in my room;" "I lazed away more time on the sofa than you in all your life." The image, cumulatively painted by these lines, is a quite physical one: a body on a sofa, sloth-like, idle, unproductive. And it will, of course, be familiar to any Kafka reader, since it duplicates his most famous creation: insectoid Gregor Samsa laid up wriggling on his back, "curtaining and confining" himself in his room, shamefully failing to emerge, go out to work and earn some money for his family. "But" (you might say) "this is different, since, while Gregor just degenerates, the sofa-dwelling Kafka here is reading books, educating himself, learning how to write." Yet Kafka is himself at pains to disabuse his father of his earlier illusion that his son's withdrawal-enclave is a "productive" one, a space of profitable intellectual endeavor. "If you had any real idea," he tells him, of how "minute" the "total achievement in work done" at home, as at the office, was, "then you would be aghast;" the "total sum" of wisdom he has acquired over the years "is extremely pitiable in comparison with the expenditure of time and money." The intellectual zone, it seems, zone of the writer, far from being a positive alternative to that of normal labor and production, is a wasteful and profligate space of negative equity, no more auspicious or autonomous than Gregor's pitiable kingdom. A degenerative logic binds the act of writing to the shameful body, wiring both into the same auto-consumptive feedback loop: Kafka's surprise at having good digestion causes him to lose it, and the hypochondria that follows gives rise to TB, which is exacerbated by the damp conditions of the apartment he hires in the Schönbornpalais "which, however, I needed only because I believed I needed it for my writing, so even that comes under the same heading."

THAT *DIGESTIVE* PROBLEMS open Kafka's illness-floodgates seems significant. *Letter* is full of eating, mouths being fed. At table, the father "ate everything fast, hot and in big mouthfuls," cracking bones with his teeth, telling his children to "Eat first, talk afterwards . . . Faster, faster, faster." As a child, Kafka "was so unsure of everything that in fact I possessed only what I actually had in my hands or in my mouth or what was at least on the way there." Later, when studying law, he feels he is "living, in an intellectual sense, on sawdust, which had, moreover, already been chewed for me in thousands of other people's mouths," adding that this is, after all, "to my taste." Orality is everywhere, a general condition—so much so that its literal stage, the dining table, is like a parliament or (to use Wiener's term again) governor's mansion from which an entire territory is administered, the seat where power is consolidated and, perhaps, might also be contested. Noting that his father doesn't obey his own table rules, Kafka has a vision of the world divided into three parts: "one in which I, the slave, lived under laws that had been invented only for me and which I could, I did not know why, never completely comply with; then a second world, which was infinitely remote from mine, in which you lived, concerned with government, with the issuing of orders and with annoyance about their not being obeyed; and finally a third world where everybody else lived happily and free from orders and from having to obey." Kafka's political options are thus threefold: either to obey the orders, which is disgraceful "for they applied, after all, only to me"; or to defy them, which is disgraceful too (how dare he?); or to *fail* to obey through lack of strength and skill and appetite— which is, if anything, still more disgraceful.

These oral battlefields, then, these set-tos of orality, produce no overthrow of power, no outbreaks of what Kafka elsewhere in *Letter* dismissively calls "violence and revolution." Rather, they perpetuate disgrace. Not revolution but revolt. They do so at the most visceral level. The father constantly voices his disgust, denounces the food as "uneatable," calls it "this swill," claims that "'that brute' (the cook) had ruined it," admonishes the children not to make a mess on the floor even as the floor beneath his seat amasses more food scraps than any other spot. This language of disgust extends to other contexts: Irma, placed in the father's care and employ, is decried by him as "a damned mess to clear up;" Kafka's short-lived interest in Judaism "'nauseated' you" (Kafka hammers this term home four lines later with the quasi-repetition "nausea"). From a cybernetic perspective, could nausea—vomiting or reflux—be viewed as a corrective? An emetic, certainly. As *Letter* draws on, an emetic tendency emerges and grows larger and more urgent, a sense on the part of the father that his *oikos* needs to be protected from or to reject impurities, infection, "filth." Advising his son on the sexual disease-preventing benefits of prophylactics as they walk together on the Josefsplatz ("near where the *Länderbank* is today"), the father wants "to see to it that physically [*körperlich*] speaking I [the son] should not bring any of the filth home with me...you were only protecting yourself, your own household." The upshot of this exchange is that the father, in remaining "a pure man, exalted above these things," with "almost no smudge of earthly filth on you at all," ends up "pushing me, just as though I were predestined to it, down into this filth...so if the world consisted only of me and you, a notion I was much inclined to have, then this purity of the world came to an end with you and, by virtue of your advice, the filth began with me."

It's an astonishing passage, an astonishing exchange—no less so for taking place, as Kafka deliberately points out, next to what both father and son can now recognize as an economic signifier: a spot that would, quite literally, become a bank. Kafka may have earlier expressed a wish, if not "to fly right into the middle of the sun" when founding his own *oikos*, at least "to crawl into a clean little spot on the earth where the sun sometimes shines and one can warm oneself a little." Yet, as he discovers, his destiny is not to find a clean spot but rather to be pushed down into the filthiest, most lowly earth-lair (or burrow) of all. From here on, it's all worms, and vermin, parasites "which not only sting but, at the same time, suck the blood, too, to sustain their own life." For "vermin," Kafka uses *Ungeziefer*, the same word he'll use for Gregor lying beneath dirt-streaked walls amidst "balls of dust and filth," with "fluff and hair and remnants of food ... on his back and along his sides." Like Gregor, or like K. running his office or "dirty household" from the squalor of a squatted classroom, Kafka will found his *oikos*, set up shop, *in the filth*. It will be a shadow-hearth, a default- or defaulting shop—but it will operate. "Unfit," as he has his father tell him in *Letter*'s most vicious feedback-instance, its final, ventriloquized riposte, "for life," he will nonetheless, perversely, find a way "to settle down in it comfortably."

And central to that finding, to that operation, to that perverse comfort, will be the practice and act of writing: shameful, negative, degenerate, insect-like—as witness this very letter, in which he reenacts the very parasitism, the bad economic practice, of which he is guilty by accusing his father of it ("you," Kafka has his father "answer" him, "prove that I have deprived you of all your fitness for life and put it into my pockets" where in fact "you calmly lie down and let yourself be hauled along through life, physically and mentally, by me"). If marrying presents the irresolvable co-nundrum of the escaping prisoner rebuilding his own prison, writing is no more effective a "leave-taking" from his father's dominion, since the former merely reproduces the latter, *in* and *as* writing: "My writing," he confesses, "was all about you." In writing, Kafka is "reminiscent of the worm that, as a foot tramples on the tail end of it, breaks loose with its top end and drags itself aside." All boys, all sons, have done that to a worm at some point in their lives. What does the worm do next? It burrows down into the earth and sets up its diminished store there once again. *Letter* is a mise-en-scène of that regressive, quivering movement or moment of burrow-formation, and, as such, catastrophically fuckuptive though it may be, enacts the primal scene and very possibility of a literary body that (with the exception perhaps only of Joyce's) would turn out to be the most extraordinary—and, ultra-paradoxically, extraordinarily successful—of the twentieth century.

In *METAMORPHOSIS*, it's not just crumbs and scraps that lie round Gregor's room and stick to his back; it's whole meals too, passed through him in unchanged condition. As his sister points out, "The food came out again just as it went in"—undigested. In one vital aspect, *Letter* is like that food: Kafka prepared it, and delivered it to his mother, who was supposed to play post-lady and forward it to his father. But this never happened; instead, it found its way, unread, to Max Brod, and so on to us. Thus it, too, is, in a way, withheld; rather than being digested by its addressee, its contents processed, broken down, it remains lying around, a shameful object, *Stoff* unabsorbed by the cybernetic (or enzymatic) architecture of the postal system, comprehension, time. Even a hundred years on—pungent, revolting, and exquisite—it repeats on us.

2015

The Geometry of the Pressant

ALAIN ROBBE-GRILLET DIED WHILE I was writing this essay. The obituaries he received in the British press depicted him as a significant but ultimately eccentric novelist whose work foreswore any attempt to be "believable" or to engage with the real world in a "realistic" way. In taking this line, the obituarists displayed an intellectual shortcoming typical of Anglo-American empiricism, and displayed it on two fronts: firstly, in their failure to understand that literary "realism" is itself a construct as laden with artifice as any other; and secondly, in missing the glaring fact that Robbe-Grillet's novels are actually ultra-realist, shot through at every level with the sheer *quiddity* of the environments to which they attend so faithfully. What we see happening in them, again and again, is space and matter inscribing themselves on consciousness, whose task, reciprocally, is to accommodate space and matter. As Robbe-Grillet was himself fond of declaring: "No art without world."

This type of intense congress with the real can be seen even in Robbe-Grillet's shortest offerings. In the three-page story "The Dressmaker's Dummy" (which opens the collection *Snapshots*), we are shown a coffeepot, a four-legged table, a waxed tablecloth, a mannequin and, crucially, a large rectangular mirror that reflects the room's objects—which include a mirror-fronted wardrobe that in turn redoubles everything. Thus we are made to navigate a set of duplications, modifications and distortions that are at once almost impossibly complex and utterly accurate: this is how rooms actually look to an observer, how their angles, surfaces and sightlines impose themselves on his or her perception. No other action takes place in the piece, which nonetheless ends with a quite stunning "twist" as we are told that the coffee-pot's base bears a picture of an owl "with two large, somewhat frightening eyes" but, due to the coffeepot's presence, this image cannot be seen. What waits for us at the story's climax, its gaze directed back towards our own, is a blind spot.

In *Jealousy*, this blind spot is the novel's protagonist. Through a meticulously—indeed, obsessively—described house set in the middle of a tropical banana plantation moves what filmmakers call a POV or "point-of-view," a camera and mic-like "node" of seeing and hearing. The one thing not seen or heard by this node is the node itself. Phrases such as "it takes a glance at her empty though stained plate to discover..." and "Memory succeeds, moreover, in reconstituting..." beg the questions: Whose glance? Whose memory? The answer, it can pretty easily be inferred from the novel's context, is that it is the master of the house's glance and memory, his movements and reflections we are experiencing as he watches his wife, identified only as "A...," negotiate an affair with the neighboring plantation owner, Franck. The effect of stating the hero's subjectivity negatively, by implication rather than affirmation, is eerie and troubling: his gaze becomes like that of "The Shape" in John Carpenter's *Halloween*, or the entity in David Lynch's *Lost Highway* who stalks a maritally troubled house at night armed with a camera. When we read that "it is only at a distance of less than a yard" that the back of A...'s head appears a certain way, we realize with a shudder that her jealous husband is creeping up on her from behind. He is observing her, in this particular instance, through the slats of a blind (or *jalousie* in French); and we, through an ingenious if untranslatable linguistic duplication, are watching her through two *jalousies*: a double-blind.

The novel is saturated with a sense of geometry. The house's surfaces reveal themselves to us in a series of straight lines and chevrons, horizontals, verticals and diagonals, discs and trapezoids. The banana trees, as green as jealousy itself, are laid out in quincunxes, as are the workers who replace the bridge's rectangular beams. Geometric order is pitted against formlessness and entropy: on the far side of the valley, towards Franck's house, is a patch in which the narrator tells us, using language reminiscent of Othello's, that "confusion has gained the ascendancy." As A . . . combs her hair, the struggle between geometry and chaos is replayed: with a "mechanical gesture" the oval of the brush and straight lines of its teeth pass through the "black mass" on her head, imposing order on it, just as the "mechanical cries" of nocturnal animals shape the darkness beyond the veranda by indicating each one's "trajectory through the night." Geometry usually wins: even the "tangled skein" of insects buzzing round the lamp reveal themselves, when observed at length by the husband, to be "describing more or less flattened ellipses in horizontal planes or at slight angles." But an ellipse is not merely a type of orbit; it also designates a syntactical omission, a typographic gap. What's missing from this geometry is A . . . , the character whose very name contains an ellipse: during this particular scene she is off in town with Franck. As the narrator waits for her to come home, the lamp hisses, like a green-eyed monster.

Enmeshed with the book's spatial logic is a temporal one. The second time we see the shadow of the column fall on the veranda it has lengthened in a clockwise direction, the geometry of the house effectively forming a sundial. In a filmed interview with curator Hans Ulrich Obrist (Robbe-Grillet's influence on contemporary visual art is enormous), Robbe-Grillet ponders Hegel's paradox that to say "Now it is day" cannot be wholly true if, a few hours later, one can equally truthfully declare "Now it is night," and notes that, for Hegel, the only true part of both statements is the word "now." Why? Because it persists. The same word punctuates *Jealousy* like the regular chime of a clock: "Now the shadow of the column ..."; "Now the house is empty..."; "...until the day breaks, now."

This is not to say that time moves forwards in a straight line. Like Benjy in William Faulkner's *The Sound and the Fury*, *Jealousy*'s narrator experiences time—or times—simultaneously. For Robbe-Grillet, who also made films, writing is like splicing strips of celluloid together to create a continual present. There are prolepses, analepses, loops and repetitions (a process slyly mirrored in the staggering of the plantation cycle through the whole year such that all its phases "occur at the same time every day, and the periodical trivial incidents also repeat themselves simultaneously")— but the time is always "now." A delightful exchange between the husband and the serving boy, in which the latter answers a question as to when he was instructed to retrieve ice cubes from the pantry with an imprecise "now" (discerning in the question "a request to hurry"), carries this point home: all the book's actions and exchanges swelter in a stultifying, oppressive and persistent present tense—what Joyce, in *Finnegans Wake*, calls "the pressant."

The only escape route from this "pressant," from its simultaneity, its loops and repetitions, would be violence: for the narrator to perpetrate a *crime passionel* against A . . . and, by murdering her, free them from the vicious circle of meals, cocktails, hair combing, spying. But this does not happen. Only the centipede dies: again and again and again. The venomous *Scutigera* serves as a meeting point for associations so overloaded that if it were a plug socket it would be smoking. During one of its many death scenes the narrative cuts from the crackling of its dying scream as its many legs curl to the crackling sound made by the many teeth of A . . .'s brush running through her hair; then on to A . . .'s fingers clenching the tablecloth in terror; from there to the same gesture played out across the bedsheet; then, finally, to Franck "jolting" and "driving" violently—a sexual image that resolves itself into a putative crash in which Franck's burning car makes the bush crackle. As with Franck's car crash, posited and then erased, it seems that A . . . has finally met a violent fate when, near the novel's end, we're shown a "reddish streak" running from the bedroom window to the veranda. But no sooner is it outlined than we are told that it "has always been there," and that A … has decided it will not be painted out "for the moment." So the moment, the eternal "now," persists, and she returns to sit at her desk as before.

A … is a fantastic creation, a *femme fatale* to rival Lady Macbeth or Clytemnestra in terms of her castrating potency. Throughout the book, Robbe-Grillet associates her with the color green ("green eyes … green irises") and coldness: she serves ice cubes "each of which imprisons a bundle of silver needles in its heart." A twist rears its head when, after she and Franck return from their night in a hotel, she taunts Franck (whose sexuality has been associated with car engines from the outset) by saying: "you're not much of a mechanic, are you?"—words that cause him to grimace. Later, as they sit side by side, our attention is diverted to the metal ice-bucket, "its lustre already frosted over." If A … retreats from the narrator, she retreats from Franck as well, remaining inaccessible to both. Perhaps the literary female she resembles most is another A … : Faulkner's Addie Bundren in *As I Lay Dying* who, despite marriage and an extramarital affair, abides "refraining" and "recessional" beyond the reach of both husband and lover, and of words themselves. As *Jealousy* nears its end A …, like Addie, slips away into the "blank areas" of the book's geometry, spending more and more time "outside the field of vision," as though commandeering the narrator's blind spot for herself.

One of A ...'s main activities throughout the novel is to read and write. She and Franck use a novel, which they have both read and the narrator has not, as a cover to discuss their own situation right in front of him. They also exchange letters. The small spasms and convulsions of A ...'s hair as she sits at her writing table, busy hands hidden from view, lend the act of writing a sexual aura by implying that she could as easily be masturbating as "erasing a stain or a badly chosen word." In this respect, there is something utterly perverse—doubly perverse—about her husband's perusal of her writing's residues, the fragments of letters left on the writing-case's blotter. These, too, are geometric figures: "tiny lines, arcs, crosses, loops, etc."—but, unlike the centipede whose form is marked so legibly across the wall (before being erased and re-inscribed, over and over again), here "no complete letter can be made out, even in a mirror"; the text remains illegible.

In the same interview with Obrist, Robbe-Grillet claims that, whereas the novels of Balzac or Dickens do not require readers since they perform all the latter's work themselves, his own writing calls for active readers who will piece it all together. It is like an Airfix kit—or, more precisely, an IKEA one, since there is always one vital piece missing. The final letter we see A ... reading has come not from Franck but rather in "the last post from Europe," from an unknown correspondent. As she sets a blank leaf on her green blotter, removes her pen's cap and bends forward to start writing, one more twist emerges: within the self-reflexive geometries of Robbe-Grillet's hall of mirrors, the ultimate blind spot might just be the reader.

2008

Stabbing the Olive
Jean-Philippe Toussaint

I.

FOR ANY SERIOUS FRENCH WRITER who has come of
age during the last thirty years, one question imposes itself
above all others: What do you do after the *nouveau roman*?
Alain Robbe-Grillet, Claude Simon, *et compagnie* redrew
the map in terms of what fiction might offer and aspire to,
what its ground rules should be—so much so that wrestling
with their legacy can be as stifling as it is exhilarating. Michel
Houellebecq's response has been one of adolescent rejection—or, to use the type of psychological language that the
nouveau romanciers eschew so splendidly, "denial": writing
in *Artforum* recently, he claimed never to have finished a
Robbe-Grillet novel since they "reminded me of soil cutting."
Other legatees, such as Jean Echenoz, Philippe Oster, and
Olivier Rolin, have come up with more considered answers,
ones that, at the very least, acknowledge an indebtedness—
so much so that their collective corpus is sometimes tagged

with the label "*nouveau nouveau roman.*" Foremost among this second group, and bearing that quintessentially French distinction of being Belgian, is Jean-Philippe Toussaint.

Born in 1957, Toussaint was out of the blocks quickly: by the age of thirty-five he'd published four novels, all with Minuit. It's the last of these, *La Réticence*, which most blatantly betrays his generation's haunting by its predecessor. With its off-season fishing village setting, its quasi-repeating narrative loops that see an eminently unreliable narrator cut and retrace circuits through the corridors of a hotel or to and from the house of an absent friend-cum-rival whom he may or may not have murdered, in the obsessive attention that it pays to surfaces and objects, or the geometric pulsing of a lighthouse's "*cône fulgurant de clarté*" through the black night, over and over—in all these, the book reads like an apprentice's studied emulation of Robbe-Grillet's masterpiece *The Voyeur*. The paradox is that, when *La Réticence* came out in 1991, Toussaint already had three well-received, quite differently styled books under his belt. It's almost as though, having successfully completed the first stretch of his career, he'd decided to go back and write an *homage* or pastiche, a finger-exercise to reassure himself that he could "do," straight-up, a genre that he'd been transforming from the get-go.

He'd been transforming it though the addition of an element that Robbe-Grillet and Simon's work, for all its great-

ness, lacks almost entirely: humor. The protagonists (all
nameless) of *The Bathroom* (1985), *Monsieur* (1986) and
Camera (1989) are essentially slapstick heroes in the Keaton-
Chaplin mould. They amble through the modern urban
landscape, amusing themselves by triggering and re-triggering
an automatic doorbell, flirting with a pretty secretary, or
failing to observe the etiquette and protocol of a posh
tennis club or dinner with the girlfriend's parents, to master
the workings of cars or the rules of the Highway Code. The
affect, here, stems from the naive individual's skewed encounter with systems larger than himself, an encounter
which, reprised again and again, perfectly plays out Bergson's
first rule of comedy: that life should be reshaped into a
self-repeating mechanism (it's no coincidence that so much
slapstick involves cars: in Bergsonian terms, auto-mobiles
are auto-matically funny).

What this aesthetic shares with its uncomedic *nouveau
roman* forebears is an anti-naturalist, anti-humanist bent:
reading the books, we're being given access not to a fully-
rounded, self-sufficient character's intimate thoughts and
feelings as he travels through a naturally-underpinned world,
emoting, developing and so on—but, rather, to an encounter
with *structure*. In a wonderful sequence in *Camera*, Toussaint
sets up a dialogue scene in a restaurant and, having placed
a bowl of olives on the table (as a naturalist writer would to

lend the setting background verisimilitude), suppresses the scene's dialogue entirely, preferring to describe exclusively the movement of hands as they reach towards the bowl, the flight-trajectory of fruit from hand to mouth, the ergonomics of pit-transfers down from mouth to tablecloth and, most strikingly of all, the regularly spaced imprints made by the back of a fork's tines across the skin of the lone olive the narrator toys with before stabbing it. We don't want plot, depth or content: we want angles, arcs and intervals; we want pattern. Structure *is* content; geometry is everything.

In *The Bathroom*, this logic frames the entire book, which, prefaced by Pythagoras's rule about the square on the hypotenuse being equal to the sum of the other two sides' squares, assumes a triangular form, its three sections entitled Paris, Hypotenuse, Paris. When the hero, in a willed narrative refusal to go out into the world and make something happen, takes to his bathroom and decides to stay there, he luxuriates in the tub's parallel sides and in the patterns formed by towel-rails and washing wire, as though the surfaces of space itself were like the tine-pressed olive, embossed with evenly spaced lines. Watching his lover move around their flat, he discerns the "lengthy curves and spirals" described by her arms. We exist and assume subjectivity to the extent that we occupy a spot in or traverse the grid: an implicit philosophical assertion that's part Descartes, part

Deleuze. Geometry is not just an aesthetic: it is, to borrow a term from Deleuze, our "habitus." When the narrator finally leaves the bathroom and the flat whose passages he's "stalked" (shoes intercepting shafts of light, half-open doors on each side providing symmetry and rhythm), he travels in the boxed cube of a train compartment to a Venetian hotel, there to install himself in a new bathroom, to stalk new hallways, both of which he describes in careful detail. His lover, joining him, tries to entice him out to view Renaissance *oeuvres d'art*, but he's not interested. Pictures and sculptures can't be inhabited, unlike the neutral, unanimated surfaces and planes of corridors and doorframes.

At one point *The Bathroom*'s hero even buys himself a dartboard, "sober-looking" and "concentric," and, drawing on a round table columns representing different countries, plays out a darts "World Cup"—alone, of course. There are echoes here of Joris-Karl Huysmans's Des Esseintes, who eschews the countries of the world in favor of their simulacra. But Toussaint's is a next-generation decadent: where Des Esseintes's stand-ins convey smells, sounds, and colors of the landscapes they replace, Toussaint's narrator has excised all mimesis: his world in absentia has been reduced to a shorthand cartography, the dartboard's intersections and the rounded chart beneath it: abstract globes made up of characterless vectors. And it's into, through, or out of these that *The Bathroom*'s single genuine "event" leaps: as his lover stands beside the board nagging him once more to get up off his ass and visit Venice, the narrator, quite deliberately, throws a dart into her forehead, piercing it as though it were an olive's skin. This, perhaps, is the *nouveau roman*'s greatest legacy: an understanding of what renders space meaningful. It's an understanding that Greek tragedy (with its houses, cities, and whole states founded on primal murders) also displays—and one, we should note in passing, which illustrates why Houellebecq is so wrong about Robbe-Grillet's writing. What we're seeing, in *The Bathroom* as in *The Voyeur*, is space being brought into its own, made present in the only true way possible: through acts of violence.

II.

In his Venetian hotel room, *The Bathroom*'s narrator watches TV with the sound off, gazing, *à la* Ballard, at "its procession of silent and incomprehensible images of disaster"—another line-crossed surface studded with violent moments. Incomplete ones, as it turns out: "Vision alone, without sound," he muses,

> is incapable of expressing horror. If the last moments of the ninety billion men who've died since the world began

could be recorded visually—filmed, put together and shown in a cinema—the sight might soon become wearisome. But if the sound of the last five seconds of their lives, their final sufferings, their gasps and cries and death rattles, could be dubbed on to one tape and played at full strength...

The passage betrays another literary influence, one perhaps as important for Toussaint as Robbe-Grillet and co: Beckett, whose haunting line spoken by *Godot*'s Vladimir—"The air is full of our cries"—it (I imagine knowingly) reprises. The difference is that Toussaint's "air" has to be understood in all its senses. His fifth book, *La Télévision*, takes the modern kind of air—air-time—as its central subject. It does this with wonderfully comic inversion: the hero decides at the novel's outset to stop watching television completely—which, of course, makes him obsessed with it. Staring for hours at his extinguished set, he reads the TV listings, or looks out of his window at the banked rows of his neighbors' screens changing the color of the night as they "flood" space, just like *La Réticence*'s lighthouse beam. Visiting a flat in which a television is playing, he tries facing it with closed eyes, then creating his own narratives by listening to the sound while watching something else. The whole city (in this case, Berlin, with its distinctive *Fernsehturm*) becomes a television: the security room of an art museum with its CCTV monitors; a fish tank; the pixelated mosaic tiling of an empty swimming pool, or the light flickering around the hero as he swims up and down a full one; the "chiaroscuro" of his own apartment. Television is the font and foundation of all our dwelling; being without a TV is, in essence, as the hero soon discovers, being without a household, since the three percentile of the European population who don't own one "is for the most part made up of bums, street people, delinquents, prisoners, loners and the mentally ill."

Boxes and boxes: again and again, the spaces Toussaint's heroes occupy take on the characteristics of media devices. *Camera*'s protagonist draws rectangles on the moist window panes of a dark driving school office, "here a large angle delimiting in space a view of buildings side by side, there a tight framing that isolated a single car, a single person walking on the sidewalk." The room itself thus functions as a photographic mechanism—a *camera* in both senses of the word—snatching moments from their contexts, creating a framework for the world's temporary arrest, and for reflection. This, for Toussaint, is the real object of all mediation: thought. Sitting in a photo booth, and finding its conditions "perfect...for thinking," the same narrator recalls the rain that he was watching, seconds earlier, move through a "shining cone of light to the neighboring darkness":

> Rain seemed to me to represent the course of thought, transfixed for a second in the light and disappearing the very next second to give way to itself. For what is the act of thinking—if it's not the act of thinking about something? It's the flow of thought that is so beautiful, yes, the flow, and its murmur that travels beyond the world's clamour.

Water and thought go hand in hand throughout his work—Toussaint is a damply pensive writer. *The Bathroom*'s hero, watching rain falling outside the flat, experiments, in the manner of his television-fixated counterpart, by first fixing his gaze on a still point and watching drops fall past it (a strategy that "doesn't convey any idea of finality"), then following each drop as it moves ineluctably towards the ground (which "demonstrates that motion, however swift it may seem, tends essentially towards immobility, and thus, however slowly it may sometimes appear to do so, continually conducts bodies towards death. Olé."). In Venice, as he gives his lover a watch, there's a kind of time-lapse vision of the movement of the canal: "The water halted for a moment round the steps of a church, then cascaded away from them one by one." Life is a Heraclitan flow that thought, constantly negotiating terms with time, tries to frieze-frame, however briefly, before releasing it once more to run its course back into oblivion's dark liquid mass.

At the same time, as anyone who's read their Barthes knows, photographs can only ever be *of* death. Toussaint, who also makes and exhibits photographic work, is very conscious of this. *Camera*'s hero, finding himself surrounded by a literal dark liquid mass as he travels on a night ferry from England, steals a fellow tourist's camera and throws it overboard—but not before snapping a few random shots himself, which, developed later, seem to reveal to him "the whole stretch of stillness that precedes life and that follows it." Thought, and its material extension in the form of technological media, are double-edged swords: attempting to create an interval of *chiar* in death's endless *oscuro*, they merely succeed in framing and reproducing the whole process by which darkness triumphs. Art—for which all Toussaint's media are to some extent stand-ins or metaphors—provides a snapshot of our condition, making it repeat, or replay, itself all over again by doing so. Even *Monsieur*, Toussaint's weakest novel, manages to make this point emphatically. Rain drenched and automobile-centered like *Camera*, it elevates its protagonist from Everyman who ponders

Schroedinger's "dead cat" paradox (that observing the be-
havior of photons makes them behave the way they do) to
comically degraded deity who sits above the world in his
high-rise office at Fiat's headquarters opening and closing
his eyes—as though he himself, like a camera, or God, were
causing light to follow darkness, then give way again. "*Fiat
lux*," writes Toussaint, punning metaphysically. The book
ends with a blackout during which, all over Paris, lamps of
passing cars and flickering cigarette lighters provide just
temporary relief. *Godot* again: as Pozzo says, "The light
gleams an instant, then it's night once more."

III.

An endearing characteristic of Toussaint's work is the way
it unashamedly reprises scenes, situations and set pieces from
one novel to the next. Cones of light, swimming pools,
aquaria, octopi, chess games, lovers observed while opening
letters, photographs and phone-boxes, to name but a few
Toussaintean motifs, recirculate with a rhythm that's fresh
and new in the very boldness of its repetition: the books,
like *Camera*'s narrator says of his own life, seem to be "moving forward, yes, in a constant renewal of identical wavelets."
A structural setup that Toussaint is fond of is the triangular
one: start in Paris; take a trip somewhere else and stay in a

hotel; go back to Paris. In the early novels, that "somewhere else" is usually Italy, sometimes London or Cannes, but always European. In his more recent diptych *Faire L'Amour* and *Fuir*, published in 2002 and 2005 respectively, it's the Far East.

Monsieur's protagonist wondered whether, given Earth's rotation, one could move east in order to escape oneself—yet what his successor in the Eastern novels is escaping is time. Or perhaps half-escaping: arriving in an alien time-zone, his body clock as out of synch as his wristwatch's redundant hands, the narrator of these books ("the same character," I'd write, if all Toussaint's nameless subjects weren't the same—or, rather, if his whole oeuvre didn't constantly renew the same question of subjectivity itself) finds that jetlag has granted him a kind of a fold, bubble, or indentation that allows him to occupy time differently. This is an ontological, not psychological, phenomenon. As the hero points out in *Fuir*, jetlag causes "a slight distortion in the fabric of reality, a shift, a misalignment…" There's a shift in the writing in the Eastern novels too—an upward one—as old shaft-teeth interlock with those of a new gear-plate, giving a familiar engine more purchase. The Tokyo of *Faire L'Amour*, like *Télévision*'s Berlin, becomes a TV set, but a richer and sharper model, with data units flickering over every surface as hotel windows reflect ubiquitous traffic lights and neon signs, producing "*indéchiffrables colonnes d'idéogrammes.*" People become data-impregnated screens as well, with illuminated ciphers sliding across their shirts and cheeks as they amble through street markets. Viewed from a tower twice as high as Fiat's, the nocturnal Eastern city doesn't require substitution by an abstract grid, since it already is one. And, once more, it's from this grid itself that the violent event comes: as the hero and his lover wander through a night they hope will never end, a heavy earth tremor brings space juddering to life.

Before leaving the hotel, the narrator (naturally) swims in its top-floor pool and, thoughts merging with the water, tells us that "I myself was time's flow." *Faire L'Amour* and *Fuir* are as Heraclitan as the rest of Toussaint's novels; but in *Fuir* the flow takes on a much more proairetic character. Dispatched to Shanghai by Marie, the same *femme fatale* with whom he wandered through the flickering Tokyo markets in the last book, the hero hands a package of whose contents he's uncertain to a contact he knows nothing about, then is whisked off to Beijing by a second sexy woman, whereupon the three of them (the contact has come along, package secreted in his shirt) are chased by police from bowling alley to building site to bar in a fast-paced action sequence with grand, universal overtones. The effect, in terms of the prose, is quite hilarious—like reading a James Bond novel penned by Beckett rather than Ian Fleming:

We came flying out into this world without shifting gears, still rushing ahead, still tense, still in a state of shock, running away, our bodies trembling, still feeling the urge to escape, having trouble controlling the bike, braking, hitting the sidewalk too fast, with too much force...

Another way in which the Eastern novels differ from their predecessors is in the priority they give to that bugbear of all things even vaguely avant-garde: relationships. For all their narrative refusal and machinic logic, Toussaint's first three novels also involved emotional encounters between men and women. They could even be seen as playful renditions of quite conventional romantic situations—but only if reengineered through reading, in the same way as some student guides to *Ulysses* try to persuade us that what's "really" going on in such and such a scene is Bloom pining for Molly, for example (*No*, I always want to shout out when I read those, *what's really going on is tramlines vibrating, soap singing and language rioting, just like it says!*). But *Faire L'Amour* and *Fuir* are unabashedly "about" the troubled love between the hero and his girlfriend. As he cavorts with the second, Chinese woman in the toilet of a hurtling train in the latter novel, the strange contact-figure brings a ringing mobile phone to him, and he hears Marie's distant and distraught voice saying her father has just died. There's mediation, time-lapse, speed and death (doubly so: as she leaves the Louvre, where she's calling from, Marie passes a car crash on the Rue de Rivoli)—but also straight-up, almost sentimental pathos. The last section of the novel sees the narrator return to Europe to attend the father's funeral in Elba, the phone—and, indeed, all mediation—becoming quite redundant as he rejoins his love in person.

Is there a retro-move going on here? A crypto-reactionary step back towards humanism, sentimentalism, positivism, and the whole gamut of bad *isms* that the vanguard twentieth-century novel has expended so much effort overcoming—a back-step, moreover, carried out through the deployment of some of that very vanguard's own techniques? It's hard to say. In *La Patinoire* ("The Ice Rink"), a film that Toussaint scripted and directed (the man is a true polymath), the French director-character (it's a film-about-the-making-of-a-film) tries to explain to his American star that he hides love stories behind elaborate formal exercises. Is that an inverse way of saying that, in order to get away with formal exercises, he uses love stories as a commercial sweetener, a Trojan horse? Either way, the star, not speaking French, smiles back and tells him "I don't understand," then, as the ice, with all its skate-scored geometry, melts beneath the spotlights, he goes off and screws the leading lady the director covets. It's a brilliantly comic moment—and one that (again) replays, or snapshots, *en abîme*, the complex cultural legacy Toussaint has inherited, and its relation to a dumb mainstream culture in a corner of whose soil it must somehow take root and grow.

IV.

To say of an artist that "it will be interesting to see where he goes from here" might be the most banal of commonplaces—yet in Toussaint's case, given the Manichean battle playing itself out in his work, it seems appropriate: will his oeuvre turn out, ultimately, to have been deconstructing literary sentimentalism or sentimentalizing literary deconstruction? I suspect he'll keep us guessing, although not through lack of productivity. In the time it's taken me to write this piece, it seems, he's managed to knock out yet another novel. The winner of the Prix Décembre (how nice of the French to give an award each month), *La Vérité sur Marie* reprises the Paris-Tokyo-Elba triangle, turning the Eastern diptych (for the moment at least) into a triptych.

It reprises plenty more: the logic and aesthetics of the TV reassert themselves as Marie's new lover, struck down by a heart attack, is wired up to monitors that translate his very life force into lines moving across a screen; the hero's coitus with a new fling is again interrupted by Marie's phone call, as it was in *Fuir*; there's rain, and geometry, and more rain. And, like a perpetual thunderstorm, the Manichean battle rages unresolved. The novel's end, which sees the hero reconciled—again—with Marie against the backdrop of a catastrophic forest fire, strikes me initially as worn—trite, even, tasting more of syrup than of soot. But this is blown away by a stunning Faulknerian sequence in the middle describing the fraught transportation of a racehorse through Narita airport. As he bolts out of his box, dragging his handlers across the rainy tarmac till they let go or are knocked unconscious, regularly spaced arc lights frame a *"tourbillon de muscles"* and the horse, readying himself to jump over the line of vehicles hemming him against the perimeter fence, threatens to turn into Pegasus. He does, in a manner: recaptured and placed in a cargo plane's hold, he ends up airborne, riven by turbulence as lightning and wing-lights flash and pulse through the surrounding darkness, a sentient thing framed in a metal box that itself lies in a metal box, armed with no more than *"la certitude d'être là"*: despite his non-human nature—or perhaps even because of it—an exemplary Toussaintean subject.

If to wonder aloud which direction a writer's future course will take is clichéd, to say of his novels that one of their best qualities is their shortness must seem like an insult, some kind of Wildean put-down. Yet this is, indeed, one of the best things about Toussaint's writing: its conciseness, its elision. All his books are short—none more so than *La Mélancholie de Zidane*, a ten-page essay that Minuit, charmingly but also quite correctly, published in 2006 as a standalone book. *Zidane* is perhaps the closest Toussaint comes to meta-fiction: in it, he not only revisits all his themes and motifs, but does this with explicit references, dropped in via footnotes, to *The Bathroom*, Gaston Bachelard and Freud. Lucky enough to have been in Berlin's Olympic Stadium on July 26, 2006 for the World Cup Final and *that* head-butt, Toussaint sees in Zidane a classic melancholia: the card he's shown is not red, he asserts, but black. Like everyone else in the ground, the author missed the incident itself (it took place off the ball), but saw it on the replay screen: always-already mediated, even for those present. If it's violence that makes space meaningful, then Zidane's act was the event *par excellence*. In Toussaint's rendition of it, the football pitch's painted lines become geometry's vectors; the ball's movement, a "*trajectoire du billiard*"; the passage of Zidane's head, "*un geste de calligraphie.*" Zidane himself, like the Narita horse (whose name, perhaps not so coincidentally, also begins with *Z*), becomes an embodiment of raw, animal consciousness in space, aware only of "*le sentiment d'être là, simplement là.*"

He also becomes, with his calligraphy and his mad "*geste

inédit," a kind of writer—and the whole episode turns into a Proustian meditation about time. Zidane, who had announced prior to the game that it would be his last one ever, wanted, Toussaint claims, to stop the ninety minutes running their full course, to short-circuit finitude itself. It's a beautiful reading of the iconic moment—and, in a more roundabout way, a fine take on literature. Toussaint ends, Zidane-like, by removing all possibility of endings in invoking yet another *Z*, Zeno: Zidane's head, he points out, cannot ever really have reached Materazzi's chest, since it would have had to travel half the distance there, then half the remaining distance, and so on to infinity—what Toussaint calls "*le paradoxe de Zidane*." Thus we're left, appropriately, in suspension: held, geometry-bound, in a space, or time, that has become pure interval.

2010

On Dodgem Jockeys[*]

IN ONE OF HIS SHORT PIECES that hovers uncomfortably between being a novel, an essay, and an exercise in clinical observation, Georges Perec muses that he's missed his true calling: rather than a writer, he should have become a controller for the Paris City Transit Authority. The revelation comes at the end of a day spent sitting in the same spot noting down (among other things) the passage of pedestrians to and from the metro and the frequency with which the variously numbered buses pass by, some full, some empty. But, more subtly, his reasoning goes as follows: if the writer's task is to record events in time; to bring into sharp focus the trajectories of human lives, both singularly and in all their crowded multiplicity, the contingencies—be these of chance or design—of a hundred, or a thousand, or a million

---

*In Britain, bumper cars are also known as dodgems. The two or three fairground employees who move between cars, riding their rear bumpers for short stretches, reaching down to take over the wheel when, for example, several cars have become wedged together, are a perennial fixture of the dodgem ring.

comings-together, transfers and leave-takings; to intuit and communicate their overall rhythm; and, beyond even that, to peer beneath their surface and reveal the fabric holding the whole thing together, unpick and reconstruct its very weft and warp—well, the transit controller does exactly this.

By the same logic, I would suggest that the most noble and heroic thing to be in this life, or perhaps in any other, is the dodgem jockey. You know what I mean: those guys who work the bumper cars in fairgrounds. Not the fat, older one who sits in the control booth—Perec's fantasy—but the lithe young things who cling to the backs of moving cars, hopping from one to the next.

Considered structurally (and what is a fairground ride but a mechanical construction?), the dodgem ring is made up of three strata. At the top, the grid—that is, speaking Cartesianly, space itself, its sublimated essence and totality; and, speaking metaphysically, the heavens, electrified domain from which the gods cast out their bolts, zap life down to the realm below. That second realm, the floor, the stage across which human dramas play themselves out with a predictable, if frenzied and excited, regularity, is, despite its footstamp-ing, wheel-grabbing aspirations to autonomy, powered by the first, which crackles from time to time with angry light-ning to remind it where the charge lies in this setup.

Dodgem jockeys, though, occupy the third stratum, the

one lying between the other two: the realm of conductivity, of conveyance. This makes them angels: messengers, or mediators, who ensure that heaven's work is carried out uninterruptedly on earth, nudging things along, sorting out blockages. In terms of volume, their zone is the biggest: where the ceiling, like the floor, is flat (even the gods are horizontal), it alone has a vertical dimension. While their nominal "patrons" are obliged to sit for the duration of the ride, they stand tall, towering, erect. Like erotic dancers swinging round their poles, these men are the stars of the show, and they know it. Each ride is a performance, a ballet whose choreography is made all the more exquisite by the casual way in which it's executed: glissades disguised as offhand sidesteps between moving vehicles, coupés as distracted shifts of weight from one foot to the other. They have mastered laws of motion not found elsewhere: dodgem cars make no distinction between forward, neutral, and reverse, but submit rather to an endless coiling of the wheel through which every direction flows out of its opposite. A quantum field, vertiginous, abyssal, in whose depths these agents of relativity hover, paradoxically enabling movement to proceed along axes and vectors postulated by old, naive laws of physics from which they themselves have long since been exempted.

The dodgem jockey, clinging uninvited to your car—*your*

one, the one you've paid, down-payed for—represents the figure of the stranger lodged within the home. He's the *Un-heimliche*, the Uncanny, stuck onto you like an incubus. What better image for the gypsy in the popular imagination, its fantasies and fears? Within the fairground, this rickety, nomadic mobile city brought to you on trucks, the bumper-car ride, mise-en-scène of rickety mobility, sits like a miniature reproduction of the whole. These men, then, restlessly moving between moving cars, replicate yet again the overall condition of nomadism: a regressiveness that partakes of infinity. Through such endless repetitions, they both multiply and merge with other quasi-folkloric characters who populate the margins of our consciousness: cowboys, for example, hired hands exhorting mutinous, anarchic herds to follow a course that, if no two of its individual paths are identical, nonetheless amalgamates to a coherent whole; or logjammers, riding the very masses they prod and corral, skipping between these as they bump and roll, teasing equilibrium from the rim of chaos; or linesmen dangling from pylons as sparks leap into the air around their heads, whispering into their ears (and only theirs) the static, white-noise secrets of the firmament.

In Paul Klee's famous painting of (and here we loop back, like a dodgem, to an earlier motif) a hovering angel, Walter Benjamin discerns not just any angel: this one, he tells us, is the Angel of History, who travels one way while facing the other, backward. Where mortals perceive a chain of separate events that amount to "progress," the angel sees one single, ongoing catastrophe that piles wreckage upon wreckage, hurling it before his feet. Are dodgem jockeys Angels of History, too? I would say: yes, they are. They've seen it all before: these circuits blurring into one, these endless crashes, disasters playing out as pleasure, roar of the generator merging with screams of girls, bellows of boys who hope to get into their pants later that night, when the ride's over, generate more generations, send more wreckage the angel's way.... They've seen the entire tapestry, its pattern. Free-floating witnesses, they were there: at your conception, and the universe's, when circulating atoms deviated and collided.

2011

Nothing Will Have Taken Place Except the Place

PICTURE THE SCENE: three men riding a Buick LeSabre south-southwest on Interstate Highway 15, returning to Los Angeles after a weekend playing the tables in Las Vegas. One of them, riding shotgun, has been trying for some time to write a novel, without much success. A second, the driver, has for some reason brought his typewriter along; lying on the leather banquette beside him, it seems to goad his passenger. Eventually, the passenger can take no more: as they race across the hottest and most barren stretch of California desert, he grabs the thing and hurls it through the open window. The car screeches to a halt; the three men, disembarking, traipse back to examine the machine's wreckage, strewn over a hundred yards of tarmac, dirt and bush. The backseat passenger whips out his camera and starts photographing the smashed parts, like a road-accident investigator; the other two, warming to the forensic aesthetic, join in the role-play, standing beside and pointing soberly at shards of line space lever assembly, holding shift balance springs up for examination, noting the flung arc of the un-spooled ribbon. Back in LA, the driver, one Ed Ruscha, collates the developed snaps and (one year later, in 1967) publishes them in limited-run book form under the title *Royal Road Test*.

Did it actually happen like this? Who knows. Numerous, often contradictory versions of the story are in circulation. Some of these suggest that the throwing and photographing were planned in advance. One, apparently approved by Rus-cha himself, hints that the plan was even typed out on the typewriter, which would thus have scripted its own destruc-tion. The confusion seems fitting: all these story fragments popping up years later, like so many twisted, chipped machine-parts that, no matter how hard anyone tries, can never quite be re-assembled or restored into a functional or "prelapsarian" whole. Yet despite its hazy origins, and through its very narrative mutations, the episode, for me, enacts, or reenacts, something of the nature of what, else-where, I've tried to describe as a "primal scene" of modern writing. Like all primal scenes, it is both catastrophic and constitutive. Catastrophic for obvious reasons: violent, de-structive, everything that comes under the Yeatsian rubric of things falling apart, centers not holding, anarchy being loosed upon the world. The branding seems significant:

rather than (say) an Olivetti, it's a *Royal* typewriter getting trashed here. Within the schema of political allegory, what we're witnessing is less defenestration than beheading, the monarch's execution by the blade, *le sabre*. Within a vaguer or more general schema, what we're seeing is *sovereignty* being shattered: the sovereignty of the subject, that is, of the autonomous, autarchic self who masters chance, seizes his destiny—and by extension, of this self in the form of the artist who masters his craft, works its machinery with delicacy and precision so as to both express himself and turn the world into a set of works that reel off his roller; and the sovereignty, I'd suggest as well, *of writing*, whose blood and guts, whose font and lettering, the very mechanism of whose possibility we encounter threshing and dying at the roadside. And (at the same time and by contrast) constitutive: because this Orphic scattering seems to fertilize the space around it, seeding it with lettered possibility. Writing, almost miraculously, starts to sprout on bushes; the landscape, both physical and cultural, seems magically altered or regenerated. The passenger's novel may never come to be written, and it's a safe bet to say that no progeny of any type will issue from that Royal—and yet, despite, indeed as a result of this disastrous event, a book of sorts, of a new or nascent order, will appear.

Three years later, in 1970, Ruscha publishes another

example of what (in part thanks to him) we now all-too-easily place within the genre of "artist's book." *Real Estate Opportunities*, consisting of twenty-five photographs of empty lots, features no broken typewriter—yet there's a continuity in the very title. The etymology of the term "real estate" is disputed: some say the "real" derives from *res*, things; others that it comes from *rex*, king, like the Spanish *real*; while "estate" can designate one's stuff, one's sovereign domain or one's condition. These photographs, like those of *Royal Road Test*, feature typographic degradation; in "Between 6033 and 6043 Hollywood Blvd, Hollywood," we see the letters of the sign announcing the Continental Sound Recording Studios car park rejigged, through decay, into

CONTI E T

SOU D

RECORD R

035 P KING

For Ruscha, space and language belong to the same category. He talks, in interviews, of his appreciation for the way that both words and landscape "happen to be horizontal, that letters follow one another with spaces and pauses and then more letters." "Streets," he tells us (as though recalling his road test's unwound spool), "are like ribbons"—which is what, in his self-titled "ribbon-word" works, words (like *The World*, *Satin* and—yes—*Royal*) turn into too. The expanses and horizons of his large-scale landscape paintings, from the red skies filled with the STANDARD signs that punctuate America right through to the alps with "BLISS BUCKET," "HISTORY KIDS" or simply "THE" plastered in front of them, he describes as no more than "anonymous backdrops for the drama of words." And this drama's plot, time and again, consists of words being damaged; indeed, one of his paintings, "Damage," shows the *A* and *G* of that word set on fire; another, "Hurting The Word Radio," depicts the letters R-A-D-I-O being clamped and pinched. His early "phrase paintings," such as "Faster Than A Speeding Beanstalk" and "Guacamole Airlines," see partial or misheard speech fragments dislodged (as the critic Mary Richards points out in her monograph on Ruscha) from their context and hung up to dry (Ruscha himself describes the amputated half-phrases as "titles for imaginary books"); the later ones, such as "Uncertain Frontier" and "Name, Address, Phone," set again to the backdrop of landscape, see the words erased entirely.

Ruscha locates his own *Eureka* moment in 1965, when he made a large-scale work called "Noise, Pencil, Broken Pencil, Cheap Western." At the top, the word "NOISE" towers in Hollywood-style letters; falling off the bottom is a cowboy comic; on the far left, an intact pencil; on the far right, a broken one (such that read in the normal way, from left to right, the painting, like *Royal Road Test*, would narrate the writing implement's destruction); in the middle, taking up most of the canvas, empty space. "The idea of a broken pencil," Ruscha says, "reminded me of a stage set, or an aerial photograph of some trivial occurrence. I mean, there are two simple, stupid objects that seemed to beg to be captured, or recorded. And the idea was doing that—capturing them and recording them, fitting them into this picture in such a way that they almost look as if they're leaving the picture. They're on the outside edges, scrambling to get away from the center of this domain that is the picture." It may be fanciful, but reading this account, I can't help hearing echoes of Auden's take, in his poem "Musée des Beaux Arts," on Breughel's *Landscape With The Fall of Icarus*—a painting whose main surface area, like that of Ruscha's, is given over to an empty, blue expanse. Musing that human dramas take place "While someone else is eating or opening a window or just walking dully along," picturing children "skating/on a pond at the edge of the wood" while "the miraculous birth" unfolds, or "the dreadful martyrdom" running its course "in a corner, some untidy spot," Auden observes:

In Breughel's Icarus, for instance: how everything turns
    away
Quite leisurely from the disaster; the ploughman may
Have heard the splash, the forsaken cry,
But for him it was not an important failure; the sun shone
As it had to on the white legs disappearing into the green
Water, and the expensive delicate ship that must have
    seen
Something amazing, a boy falling out of the sky,
Had somewhere to get to and sailed calmly on.

Icarus's fall, the event that gives rise to the picture in the
first place, may be monumental—but it is also, within the
picture, a kind of non-event. Auden famously states, in his
"In Memory of W. B. Yeats," that "poetry makes nothing
happen"—a line usually misunderstood to mean "poetry
doesn't make anything happen." But Auden's construct is
an active, positive one that casts "nothing" as an occurrence
that *takes place*. Nothing in Latin is *nihil*, as in "annihilation";
in German, *Nichts*, as in *Vernichtung*. During the Second
World War, the British Secret Service broadcast lines of
poetry into occupied France. Ninety-nine percent of these
lines were meaningless; but one in every hundred signified,
to the Resistance listeners who had the code-books, "Now

blow up the bridge. Assassinate the general—*now*." A man
or woman reads a line of poetry into a microphone in London, and in France a bridge blows up—or not. For Auden,
this would be the threat all poetry, wartime or not, poses:
each line, in the very recesses of its negation, harbors that
potentiality, that immanence (or imminence)—and poetry,
in its eventlessness, becomes (to return to his Yeats elegy)
"a way of happening, a mouth."

Ruscha believes in happening as well. "The best thing
about any creative urge, passion," he writes in a telling notebook entry, "is that it *happens*." He is also, as a second, equally
telling notebook entry shows us, fully tuned into the dual
nuances of "nothing." On the recto page he's transcribed
Lear's regal answer, as he abdicates his estate, to Cordelia's
"Nothing": "Nothing will come of nothing." On the verso,
he's written, beneath a nod to the gun-saturated work of
Raymond Chandler: "The music from the balconies nearby
was overlaid by the noise of sporadic acts of violence." In a
third diary entry Ruscha, self-confessed lover of "the violence of things" who likes to draw with gunpowder, inserts,
by means of arrows, into a blank space framing the ribbon-
word *eye*, a series of ultra-violent scenes ("killing of bank
guard," "fist fight," "practically everyone getting killed")
playing on the TV while he draws. Effectively, the arrows
work both ways, filling the space with *and* voiding it of all

these episodes. By emptying out his stretches of pictorial real estate, he loads them with potential, with (to use his own term) opportunity. It's the same in his series *Thirtyfour Parking Lots*. Resisting the temptation to unpack that single word *lot* (as fate or destiny, as portion that Cordelia's "Nothing" vies for, as leitmotif of literary modernity, from the "vacant lots" of Eliot to Pynchon's Lot 49) since it would take up this whole essay, let's limit ourselves to quoting Ruscha's own take on those famous photographs: "Architects write to me about the parking lots book, because they are interested in seeing parking lot patterns and things like that. But those patterns and their abstract design quality mean nothing to me. I'll tell you what is more interesting: the oil droppings on the ground." What animates space is the trace of what has been excluded from it: the amputation-scar of an occurrence that, in its marked absence, seeps and stains and saturates an area's surface all the more.

Michel de Certeau, in his landmark tome *The Practice of Everyday Life*, draws a distinction between "space" and "place." Place, *lieu*, becomes *espace*, space, when it is "practiced"—that is, when unlocked through the agency or tactic of a user. Georges Perec, in his fascinating text *An Attempt To Exhaust A Place In Paris*, acts as such a "user"—sitting for three days in the Place Saint Sulpice, writing down all that he sees and hears and does. "Today I'm drinking a bottle of Vittel, while yesterday I drank a coffee (in what way does that transform the square?)." *An Attempt* is full of what Perec calls "micro-events"—people meeting, traffic passing and the like—several of which seem to contain the kernels of more conventional, expanded narratives. A woman pausing by a shop window to smoke a cigarette seems like the opening to a Hitchcock film; a Brinks truck rolling by implies the entire bank-heist genre; a screaming child dragged away by two adults signals a kidnap intrigue. There are also all the building blocks of a nineteenth-century novel: over the three days of his exercise, Perec witnesses a christening, a marriage and a funeral. Whose? Doesn't matter. Neither the micro- nor the macro-blocks or kernels grow or blossom; rather, from very little, they revert—the book's whole universe reverts, as "fatigue" (again, whose? Perec's? the square's?) sets in, space darkens and empties, the text peters out—to a narrative zero. That is *An Attempt*'s great achievement: to bring things down to this zero and to hold them there, both flatlining *and* pulsing. I would claim that Ruscha pulls off the same coup in a single shot, also from *Parking Lots*: "Dodgers Stadium, 1000 Elysian Park Ave." Here, not only does he manage, by presenting one of the most charged event-spaces imaginable (a baseball field) utterly deserted, to implicitly inject it with each triumph and defeat, every 50,000-voiced roar of hope and fury and redemption from both past and future; but he also, in showing the surrounding urban transit infrastructure (the flyovers, the exit and approach roads servicing the stadium), allows this event-space to overspill its formal boundary, expanding into a whole cybernetic architecture of wider event-field, as simultaneously omnipresent and unquantifiable as that other Elysium of which Virgil writes: 'In no fix'd place the happy souls reside…They wind the hill, and thro' the blissful meadows go."

Ruscha is not the only artist interested in sport. Francis Bacon, for example, reworks press photographs of tripping footballers to recast them as soldiers stepping on land mines, turns cricketers' heads into exploding studies for his screaming pope, and so on. That sport is war by other means is a long-standing cliché; but what interests me is the third part of the triangle, poetry. Think of Virgil's predecessor Homer: there's a battle going on outside the gates of Troy, various actions, countermoves, trajectories; and this guy has to describe it. He's a commentator. A few years ago, when the Serpentine Gallery was putting on a marathon of poetry, they asked me if I'd like to do a public dialogue with some Faber-and-Faber versifier or other. No, I responded, I want to talk to the great test match commentator Henry Blofeld. Blofeld, who received a top-drawer classical education at Eton and (until he failed his midterms "by an innings")

Cambridge, not only peppers his radio broadcasts with literary allusions (groundsmen sweeping sand from wickets between innings become maids from "The Walrus and the Carpenter"), but also (as he told me when the Serpentine granted my request) measures his speech in iambic pentameters timed to the bowler's run-up. Test cricket (he reminded us) only came about in the nineteenth century because Dickens canceled a reading tour of Australia, so England sent their cricketers as cultural ambassadors instead: it's a stand-in for writing from the off. Two facts, or episodes, from Blofeld's personal history deserve a mention here. The first is that his father lent his name to Ian Fleming's James Bond villain. The second is that he (Henry) was the most promising schoolboy cricketer of his generation until almost-fatally crushed by a bus; when, covering test matches, he lauds the majesty of players in their prime, it's almost as though he were depicting his own past's future, or his future's past. What makes his commentary so good line by line, though, is the way he fills the long pauses between cricket's short bursts of action with (utterly Perecian) pigeons, clouds, vapor trails and, indeed, passing busses, all of which he manages to weave into a descriptive tapestry at whose center, always, throbs the game—all the more so in its latency or suspension.

"He grew up in some Kentucky town when all the time

and space he could imagine were equal to a playing field, some patch of striped earth bounded by plank seats." This is how Don DeLillo introduces Blofeld's American counterpart Russ Hodges, the commentator covering the National League pennant-clinching 1951 baseball game between the New York Giants and the Brooklyn Dodgers, in his 1992 novella *Pafko at the Wall* (which he would later expand into the doorstopper of a novel *Underworld*). Hodges cut his teeth doing "ghost games"—in other words, commentating from a windowless room on a game he's not at and can't see, embellishing from data sent in on a telegraph ribbon and transcribed on a typewriter into "standard baseball cryptic." "Someone hands you a piece of paper filled with letters and numbers and you have to make a ball game out of it. You create the weather, flesh out the players, you make them sweat and grouse and hitch up their pants. You construct the fiction of a distant city, making up everything but the stark facts of the evolving game." No Elysium this, but a "half-hell of desperate invention." Hodges *is* at the Giants–Dodgers game, but his commentary, of course, has the same effect of linking a space to what is outside or beyond it. "This game is everywhere. Dow Jones tickers"—those ribbons again—"are rapping out the score with the stock averages.... They're smuggling radios into boardrooms.... They got it in jail. They got it in taxicabs and barbershops.... The game and its extensions. The woman cooking cabbage. The man who wishes he could be done with drink. These are the game's remoter soul." The novella begins with ticketless boys, drawn to what DeLillo (using a variation on a term we've met before) calls "the realm of event," jumping the turnstiles, and ends with a ball being hit over the field's boundary; like Ruscha's arrows, *Pafko*'s trajectories hurl exterior things towards the inside and vice versa.

Watching the game from the stands are, among others, Jackie Gleason, Frank Sinatra and J. Edgar Hoover—seated together, the perennial unholy alliance of art, media and power. In the fifth innings, Hoover receives a private communiqué from the remote space lodged in his soul, Washington, informing him that the Soviet Union has just successfully conducted its first atomic bomb test. The news is bad, almost disastrous—but Hoover consoles himself with the thought that (thanks to his spies) Truman will announce the detonation before the Soviets do, so that "People will understand that we've maintained control of the news if not of the bomb." Politics, too, is a matter of commentating; just as the exercise of domestic control is about information-relay, mediation, capture or retrieval of not just what's on display but, even more, whatever has left the picture, doesn't want to show itself: "your hidden life," DeLillo tells his imaginary 1950s readers, "is in his" (Hoover's) "private files, all the rumors collected and indexed, the lost facts emergent." But most intriguing is the phrase DeLillo uses to summarize the message Hoover is relayed during this middle innings: "They have exploded a bomb in plain unpretending language." As with Auden's line, we need to listen to this carefully. Its apparent sense may be: "Put simply, not to beat about the bush, they have exploded a bomb"—but that's not how it's written; no, "They have exploded a bomb in [...] language." Here, we're back (at least figuratively) in the zone of British wartime poem-codes, words that make bridges blow up.

It's a theme close to DeLillo's heart. In his 1991 novel *Mao II* he has a novelist imagine typing out key-sequence detonators over phone lines: "You enter your code in Brussels and blow up a building in Madrid." This character, Bill Gray (who spent his childhood announcing ball games to himself in which he played the roles of players, commentator, crowd, audience and even radio), holds to the credo that "There's a danger in a sentence when it comes out right." At the same time, he feels emasculated, feels that writing has lost its potential for annihilation, and hence its seat at the table of world-transformation. "In the West we become effigies as our books lose the power to shape and influence...Years ago I used to think that it was possible for a novelist to alter the inner life of a culture. Now bomb makers and gunmen have taken that territory. They make raids on human consciousness. What writers used to do before we were all incorporated." Throughout *Mao II*, the figure of the terrorist acts as a counterpart to, in the dual sense of double of and replacement for, the writer. "There's a curious knot that binds novelists and terrorists . . . novelists and terrorists are playing a zero-sum game . . . What terrorists gain, novelists lose . . . The danger they" (terrorists) "represent equals our" (novelists') "own failure to be dangerous." Crediting Beckett with being "the last writer to shape the way we think and see" (which is ironic, since Beckett is the author of the work in which, as the critic Vivian Mercier famously put it, "nothing happens, twice"), Gray claims that "After him, the major work involves midair explosions and crumbled buildings. This is the new tragic narrative." If the novel used to be "the great secular transcendence," the "mass of language, character, occasional new truth," now "our desperation has led us toward something larger and darker. So we turn to the news, which provides an unremitting mood of catastrophe . . . We don't need the novel."

But Gray goes further: "We don't even need catastrophes, necessarily," he continues. "We only need the reports and predictions and warnings." The commentary is enough; the event itself is almost an afterthought; it doesn't need to actually *happen* for its field or realm to govern and survive.

This is a fundamental shake-up of the zero-sum equation: at the final tally, neither novelists *nor* terrorists win the game. Media does. The arc or trajectory along which, like a plumb-struck baseball, Trojan spear or Ruscha arrow-line, all experience finds itself cast is that of its own being mediated, its becoming-media: "Everything around us tends to channel our lives toward some final reality in print or on film," Gray claims. "Two lovers quarrel in the back of a taxi and a question becomes implicit in the event. Who will write the book and who will play the lovers in the movie?"

Here again, my maybe-fanciful ear heard a loud, clear echo—this time of a figure I've of late become obsessed with: Mallarmé. In his 1895 essay "The Book, Spiritual Instrument," Mallarmé issues his celebrated declaration that "everything that exists does so in order to end up in a book." Unlike DeLillo's Gray, though, Mallarmé is not just thinking of *a* book, of some book or other. He is picturing (as he puts it in a letter to Verlaine) "*the* book, convinced as I am that in the final analysis there's only one"—the über-book, the final, comprehensive volume, "architectural and premeditated," "the Orphic explanation of the earth." This book would be a "book" for which the very term "book" no longer sufficed, since its creation would demand the escalation and expansion—or, better put, the evisceration and reconfiguring-otherwise—of all our current notions of what books are. In the Ruscha-like notebooks in which, for the remainder of his life, he monomaniacally attempts to open approach routes to this expanded, escalated (or, to use the terminology of the century that would follow Mallarmé, many of whose artists would take up his challenge, "multi-media" or "multi-platform") book-to-come, Mallarmé imagines it being realized or enacted at a level far beyond that of the page—in (for example) performances and cult-like rituals. Yet at the same time he remains preoccupied with text, and type, and print, with the potentialities these harbor. Even in newspapers, he claims, their font and layout, we see the "miracle" of words being "led back to their origin, the twenty-six letters of the alphabet, so gifted with infinity that they will finally consecrate language; thus typography becomes a rite." The book, then, "total expansion of the letter," would harness the letter's "mobility," and in its "spaciousness" establish "some nameless system of relationships."

These ambitions and concerns run through and shape, at every level, Mallarmé's most remarkable work, *Un Coup de Des*. With eleven different type-faces and -sizes that suggest the coexisting fonts of newsprint, a non-linear spread or deconstructed layout that forces the eye to run and jump from one side of the page, one isolated word or cluster to another, and vast expanses of blank space through (and perhaps out of) which its action falls, the text recounts, in present tense, an event whose circumstances are "eternal"—that is, an episode that is both happening now and not-now-but-always. What is this episode? A *naufrage*, or shipwreck. Amid spume and surge, reef and timbers, we are shown a sinking man lifting his arm aloft to cast dice. This man, named in block capitals as "THE MASTER," would in a plot-sense be the captain of the floundering ship; in a more general sense, he embodies the general character-type of the hero, and thus, in a grander symbolic framework, of all sovereign self- or world-mastery. "Formerly," we are told, "he would grasp the helm"; but now, having drifted "beyond ancient reckonings," he finds "the manoeuvre forgotten with the age." Since the most cursory of glances through Mallarmé's previous poems uncovers numerous allusions to seafaring and seamanship, which are repeatedly set up as analogues for poetry, with Mallarmé casting himself in the role of the master ("Nothing, this foam, virgin verse . . . We navigate, O my diverse/Friends, myself already on the poop,/You the sumptuous prow to cut/Through the winter wave and lightning burst," etc), it is all but impossible to resist the urge to read *Un Coup de Des*, in part, as a gesture of abdication on the poet's part. This abdication would take the form not of a smooth handing-down of his crown, but rather of a violent destruction in which all the syntactical and metrical control, all the meticulously-wrought systems of image and allusion and conceit built up over decades, that have elevated him and his work to the masterful position they occupy, get splintered on the reef of time, modernity, and, of course, one of the poem's central motifs, chance, in its dual sense of randomness and destiny (lot). And yet, according to a paradoxical logic we should recognize by now, this catastrophic downfall breaches open and sets up, in its abyss or *gouffre*, the vanguard territory in and out of which literary modernity will take root and sprout.

Where Ruscha's buddy heaves a Royal through the window, Mallarmé's drowning master raises his hand aloft to cast dice. This, the poem suggests, would be the great tragic-heroic act, a gesture that, even from the depths of the catastrophe, would institute some kind of grasping of one's fate, a repairing or redress of falling-apartness, a suture of the whole disintegrating mechanism (the ship, literature, the age), and even a transcendence of the situation. This putative dice-cast, Mallarmé tells us, would allow the Master "to fold back division and pass proudly on." And yet the Master *doesn't* cast them. Instead, his hand remains unopened; a *plume solitaire éperdue*—lonely distraught feather or solitary overwhelmed pen (that broken pencil's cousin)—lodges in his hair; and, interspersed with lower-case snatches declaring "the event…null," "the act empty," upper-case letters shout out: "NOTHING WILL HAVE TAKEN PLACE EXCEPT

THE PLACE." For this line, the poem undergoes a tense-shift, from the present to the future-perfect: nothing *will have taken* place except the place. We also, a few lines earlier, get a shift into the conditional: even *if* the master *had* cast the dice, thereby producing a definitive outcome or "number," it still *would be* chance, and this fact would nullify the act and symbolism of the casting just as much as the not-doing of it does. In short, and simplifying a text of almost quantum levels of semantic and syntactical complexity, what we encounter, again and again, in various modes and temporalities, is the event undoing itself, disintegrating or dissolving back into the negative or neutral of its own event-space. This process plays itself out with an ineluctability that would make it seem pre-ordained, if all deity and metaphysics hadn't *also* melted down into the secular abyss of their spatial substructure. "An ordinary elevation pours out [*verse* or verses] absence": in this poem, and as poetry, un-transcendent (non-Elysian) source-fields fill all connected or contingent surfaces with emptiness; space becomes, comes into being as, its own voiding.

Pafko, in its own way, stages this situation too. At the ball-game, we are in a world of spatial relationships and kinetic mobility, of "airstreams ... coefficients ... trailing vortices." At this world's center, as the vanishing point around which it builds itself and in which it also disappears, is "that one-thousandth of a second when the bat and the baseball are in contact"—an unrecoverable, and hence abyssal, moment. "And the crowd," DeLillo writes, "is also in this lost space": they persist, the event occurs, the space itself takes place only in and as their conjoined lostness. There's also a preoccupation with chance and destiny, the vagaries (or inevitability) of how a ball will bounce and ricochet off seats as crowds fight for it (the boy who wins this micro-battle "takes a guess, he anticipates, it's the way you feel something will happen and then you watch it uncannily come to pass"). There's also, of course, a pervasive atmosphere of violence, from the smashing of a small leather sphere to the (counterpoised or corresponding) splitting of a plutonium one that causes Hoover to contemplate the ranked spectators "sitting in the furrow of destruction." As he does this, in a gesture that perfectly reprises Mallarmé's typographic sensibility, his tendency to juxtapose and collage print-blocks, a deluge of deconstructed print—of torn up magazines, thrown by the fans in the upper stands—pours down across his (Hoover's) shoulders: ads and news items and photos ("how the dazzle of a Packard car is repeated in the feature story about the art treasures of the Prado. It is all part of the same thing."). Hoover folds one of these pages up and slips it in his pocket: it's the reproduction of a Breughel, *The Triumph Of Death*, which, centered round a funnel-trap that swallows up the scene ("an oddly modern construction that could be a subway tunnel or office corridor"), depicts all space's final ruination.

Mao II also seems plugged into these Mallarméan concerns. There is not only the impetus-of-all-things-to-become-book I've already mentioned, but also, in Gray's reclusiveness and endless writer's block, his failure to put the long-awaited manuscript out in the world, the perpetually-deferred temporality of Mallarmé's to-come. There's also the intuitive link between writing and catastrophe, writing and shipwreck (or its modern counterpart, airplane-disintegration), writing and violence (in this context, the obsessive attention paid by Gray's assistant to the cogs and hammers of his typewriter makes this a good moment to mention that the Royal Typewriter Company, during World War II, also made machine guns). Reading *Mao II*, you get the sense that DeLillo is simultaneously skirting his way round a conjunction that is somehow *right*, which makes the book compelling, and not quite *getting* it right, not quite bringing the pieces into the right alignment, which makes it frustrating.

Not so Douglas Gordon and Philippe Parreno in the work I want to turn to as a coda. For their 2006 film *Zidane: A 21st Century Portrait* they have seventeen cameras track the eponymous, preternaturally gifted midfielder for the course of a football game, irrespective of whether or not he is on the ball. The game is a regular season one, in the Spanish *Liga;* Zidane's team is Real Madrid. Gordon and Parreno's title is ambiguous: on first glance, we might read it as "Zidane: A Portrait of a Subject in the 21st Century." But there's a subtler and perhaps truer grammar to be parsed here, one that would spell: "Zidane: a Portrait *of* the 21st Century, a Portrait whose subject is not really Zidane but in fact the age." And the form or manifestation that the age takes can be summed up in a single word: Media. The fundamental situation of being mediated, being-in-media, is impressed upon the viewer right from the opening sequence as, seconds into the film, the turf's green pixelates; it's reiterated in the frequent cuts to camera-feeds, the shots of edit booths, of viewing frames on monitors; it's hammered home by the way the sound drops in and out, a blatant product of technological manipulation, and by the deliberately tinny, lo-res quality of the reproduced commentary. Everything "first-hand" or "pure" is de-naturalized; even Zidane's most intimate gesture, his personal tic of scraping his foot against the grass, plays out as a kind of glitch on a CD or buffer on a livestream; it catches any fluid motion, makes it stutter, stops it happening even as it's happening. "As a child," Zidane's text-over tells us in a near-perfect paraphrase of Gray's, "I had a running commentary in my head, when I was playing. It wasn't really my own voice; it was the voice of Pierre Cangioni, a television anchor from the 1970s. Every time I heard his voice I would run towards the TV, as close as I could get, for as long as I could. It wasn't that his words were so important; but the tone, the accent, the atmosphere, was everything." For him, media is not experience's goal or endpoint, but rather its precondition, where it all begins. From that base or given, you construct your own "story" by channel-mixing inputs. Describing the crowd's sounds—general noise, the shifting of a chair, a cough, a whisper—Zidane surmises: "you can almost decide for yourself what you want to hear." Agency is editing.

The film's own editing is deconstructed: any notion that a football game might at *any* level entail some kind of organic wholeness or even machinic efficiency is constantly unraveled, as the syntax of passing, linking and sequence-formation breaks down into a set of disconnected fragments; and the human drama gives over to what we actually, at a basic perceptual level, encounter at big football games—namely, words and ciphers moving, around various centrifuges and along various vectors, through space: players' names and numbers; the team logo; or the text that, like some Jenny Holzer installation, runs in an endless horizontal ribbon along the advertisers' hoardings. (Paradoxically, the telegraph-machine in Hodges's cell was actually furnishing the truer commentary.) One of this game's main sponsors is the company Fortuna—or, in English, fate. "Sometimes," Zidane says, "when you arrive in the stadium you feel that everything has already been decided. The script has already been written." He recalls playing "in another place, at another time, when something amazing happened. Someone passed the ball to me, and before even touching it, I knew exactly what was going to happen. I knew I was going to score." What plays out on the field, (again) under the grammar of the future perfect, is replay, reenactment. Zidane's beautifully vague phrasing of "another place, another time" is apt, since the artists, like DeLillo, link their stadium's area to what's outside it. During the half-time break, they show us what is happening round the world during the game: homes destroyed by floods in Serbia-Montenegro; a spaceship recording plasmawave sounds at the solar wind termination shock boundary; a twenty-four hour marathon reading of *Don Quixote* (that seminal Renaissance study of mediation and reenactment); and, inevitably, a car-bomb exploding in Iraq. We see a still of the wounded, one of whom wears a Zidane t-shirt…

There is another fusing (to borrow Mallarmé's formulation near the end of *Un Coup*) of a place (and time) with its beyond in *Zidane*—one its authors couldn't have anticipated. The *Liga* game takes place in April 2005; the film receives its general release in September 2006. Between those two dates, Zidane is sent off in the World Cup final—as, indeed, he is in the game Gordon and Parreno have memorialized. The novelist Jean-Philippe Toussaint, who was at the fateful France-Italy encounter (and, like everyone else in Berlin's Olympiastadion, didn't see the incident, since it took place off the ball, only becoming aware of it when it was replayed on the stadium's giant screens), characterizes Zidane's general moves as "calligraphic." Calligraphy may be a good choice of allusion—yet the landmark, the epochal head-butt he performed on Materazzi was *typo*graphic. Take the faces, contexts, "personalities" away (a move that's hardly necessary, since Zidane's acephalic surrender of his head, its burial in Materazzi's chest, performs this function already); take these away and *read* the episode at a strict nomenclatural level, and what do you see? You see the two Zs, separated by seven spacing letters (which themselves contain a repetition, *ine-d-ine*), of *Zinedine Zidane*, crashing into the two compressed Zs that await them near the end of *Materazzi*, like a train hitting the buffers; themselves compressing, *ZZ* tight against *ZZ*, then springing back and spacing out again. It is perhaps the most decisive rite typography has been accorded in our era.

The alphabet's last letters, fourfolded: this, in his final game, would be Zidane's last, wordless word, his abnegation or abdication of his craft, laying-down or breaking of his pencil. His way of saying Nothing. Its utterance effects a sudden (and, for the hundreds of millions watching, for the game itself, catastrophic) *withdrawal* from the event-space that very craft has animated or brought to life in the first place. The space remains, traumatized, amputated, drawing its entire reserve (or deficit) of meaning from the presence that has just vacated it (who cares about the penalty shootout that followed? will anyone even remember who won the match in ten years time?). We see the script being typed out in the *Liga* game, as Zidane disappears, like Breughel's crowd, into the field-voiding or evacuating tunnel with three minutes left on the clock. Cordelia's "Nothing" starts a chain-reaction that will lead to war, mayhem, general armageddon. In a way, her saying of it (a speech-act that, breaking the game-rules laid down by the king, brings about her immediate withdrawal from the game) is the ultimate act of terror. After the Berlin final, some press reports suggested Materazzi had, in a racist manner, provoked Zidane into head-butting him by calling him a "terrorist"—a claim that seems to be untrue. But Zidane's Arabic heritage could be linked to the incident in a more subtle way: "The perfect act of writing," writes Giorgio Agamben, "comes not from a power to write, but from an impotence that turns back on itself and in this way comes to itself as a pure act (which

Aristotle calls agent intellect). This is why in the Arab tradition agent intellect has the form of an angel whose name is *Qualam*, Pen, and its place is an unfathomable potentiality. Bartleby, a scribe who does not simply cease writing but 'prefers not to,' is the extreme image of this angel that writes nothing but its potentiality to write." If, as Gray's assistant muses as he cleans his master's abandoned typewriter, "the withheld work of art is the only eloquence left," then space, most truly understood, would be nothing but its own potentiality, and literature its own negation. This is the two-way alchemy, the reverse-metaphysics, through which a small, dumb leather globe quite devoid of its own energy is able to at once both cancel and amass what Hoover calls "the sun's own heat that swallows cities." Or, as Zidane himself puts it (with his habitual slight stutter and repeat): "Magic is sometimes very close to nothing at all. Nothing at all."

2015

18 Semiconnected Thoughts on Michel de Certeau, On Kawara, Fly Fishing, and Various Other Things

1. SO: TRY TO SAY *NOW*. I mean, now: try to say it. Not just to say it, but to mean it too. To truly mean it: mean it in the sense of it being true. It's just not possible. No sooner has the word been formed—a peristaltic movement that breaks down into a grinding of the tongue against the wet and gummy place where palate and incisors meet, a corresponding dropping of the lower jaw, contraction of the cheeks, and curling outward of the lips (a scornful gesture, as though they, the lips, were sneering at the very content they're delivering)—no sooner has this word been manufactured and expelled than it's already late and, in its lateness, false: as its sound rises to your ears, it's not now anymore. And if you speak it once again, taking another shot, hoping

to hit it, snag its true-ness, on the rebound, then the failure is compounded; you're just consoling yourself: *Now, now.* And if you say it multiple times, over and over again in rapid-fire succession, setting up a field of pulses one of which (you hope) will coincide with one or other of the actual nows that float and slip through this same field—well, then you end up sounding like an air force corporal sending parachutists from a plane: urgent, almost hysterical: *Now! Now! Now! Now! Now!* And even then, the word unpacks itself, unfurls —each time—too late, drags languidly behind its passenger, and arrives at its destination after him as well, to crumple, as redundant as an afterthought, on indifferent ground.

2. For Ingeborg Bachmann, it's *Today* that's the impossible word. It "sends me flying into an anxious haste," she writes; pronouncing it, "my breathing grows irregular and my heart beats a syncopation which can now be captured on an electrocardiogram, although the graphs do not show that the cause is precisely my Today, always urgent and new; however, I can prove this diagnosis is correct. To use the confusing code of medicine, the disorder precedes acute phobia; it renders me susceptible, it stigmatizes me." As for the word's notation: "anything written about Today should be destroyed immediately, just like all real letters are crumpled

up or torn up, unfinished and unmailed, all because they were written, but cannot arrive, Today." The only person who should be allowed to use the term in any form, she tells us, is the suicide.

3. Yet On Kawara paints Today. Over and over again, thousands of times, in the notational shorthand of a host of languages. OCT.15, 1973. 6 MRT.1991. 1 MAR.1969. To paint a date is not to paint the contents of a day, but simply to affirm: *Today*. "This painting itself is January 15, 1966," the subtitle for *JAN.15, 1966* reads. He crafts a little box for each one of these works, its own small coffin, inside which he places a newspaper clipping from the day on which the work was painted, the Today it speaks or iterates. Why does the practice seem familiar? Who else does this? Why, kidnappers, of course: they photograph their victim holding up *The New York Times*, or have them read onto a tape: *Today, Prime Minister H. Wilson of Great Britain called on Soviet Leaders*; or, *In Sasebo, Japan, policemen battled with several hundred leftist students this morning near the main entrance to the US naval base as the nuclear-powered aircraft carrier* Enterprise *arrived*. What they're affirming, from inside the caskets in which they've been prematurely placed, is simply: *I Am Still Alive*.

4. Who has On Kawara kidnapped? The world leaders, sportsmen, astronauts, and film stars peopling his quasi-funerary newsprint hieroglyphics? (Melville's Queequeg, Richardson's Clarissa may have written on the outside of their coffins, but the Egyptians took as much care over the interiors: after all, that's where the principal reader was situated.) Or is it the bit players whom he's taken hostage: the crime victims and missing soldiers, centenarians and birth-weight-record-breaking babies? Or the extras who don't even get named: the three hundred killed by the typhoon that ravaged Tokyo, the 14,400 striking union employees of General Electric Corp, the millions who'll lose their houses in the stock-market crash? Or is it, in fact, precisely the other way round: is it, perhaps, not they but On Kawara himself who has been kidnapped? His own persona, thoughts, intentions, his experience on any given day, that is, Today, his whole reality—have these been hijacked or abducted, interned or interred, live-buried, by the paintings' formulaic and po-faced neutrality, the dates' typographic stonewall that reveals precisely nothing? No one seems to know a thing about the man. The only anecdotal tidbit that I recall ever reading about him—about *him*, that is—is that he likes fly fishing. He never goes to his own shows; never gives interviews or comments on the work; never releases photos; any of that stuff. His "biography" consists of no

more than the number of days he has clocked up: on December 15, 1991, this amounted to 21,540.

5. Fly fishing. Let's imagine him, whoever he is, doing this. The patience, the reflection (doesn't *on*, in Japanese, mean "water"?); the ongoing possibility that something might break surface, show itself—but always tempered by the fact that it's the possibility itself, not the event's occurrence, that actually animates the whole pursuit, although then *animate's* not the right word. Fills it with stillness, maybe. Fills its stillness. With what? Stillness. Yeats: "Like a long-legged fly upon the stream/His mind moves upon silence."

6. The Date Paintings each take a day to paint. If On Kawara hasn't finished one by midnight, he destroys it, since it's no longer a painting of Today. But then, of course, it's no longer a painting of Today in any case: as soon as the paint's dry, let alone by the time it's viewed, exhibited, or sold, it's already yesterday, last month, last year. And even while it's being painted, or in the few hours, or minutes, that remain till midnight, it's still not a painting of Today. "This painting itself is January 15, 1966," the painting claims, when actually the exact opposite is true: the painting is everything *but*

January 15, 1966; the essence or reality of January 15, 1966, is what has been left behind, excluded by the painting in its passage to completion, as a precondition of its permanent existence. What the painting iterates is its own time, minus the time. What has actually been kidnapped, held to ransom, by the work is time. Just like in Proust: the work sends us in search of the time that it itself has lost.

7. Is On Kawara a writer? If the answer to this question's *Yes*, then what does that make me? Certainly, he's obsessed, like any writer, by the question of narrative. *I Got Up ... I Went ... I Met ... I Read ...* These are the base units of any narrative, its opening move, Pawn to King Four gambit. He writes—rewrites, or overwrites—*The Old Man and the Sea*, reducing it to blank pages spread out to form a grid. *A novel*, continues the inscription. Could all his work be thought of as a novel? As a parenthetic, or peripatetic, epic in which On Kawara plays the role of both narrator and main character or "hero"? He's so unheroic, though. *I Got Up at 8.12 A.M.*, he reports from Oklahoma. That's it. *I Got Up at 8.29 A.M.*—from Detroit. From Mexico City: *I Got Up at 1.17 P.M.* What kept him in bed so late in Mexico City? Or we're given the route, marked out across a map, he followed through the streets of New York, Berlin, or

Quito, Stockholm, Casablanca, Freetown. What happened at the corner of Twenty-third Street and Eighth Avenue, or by the synagogue on Kungsträdgårdsgatan? The work, in its repetitiveness, its monotony, doesn't just withhold the answer; it renders the very question meaningless, irrelevant; it sacrifices its own hero, heroism itself, on the altar of monotony and repetition. On Kawara is heroically unheroic. He's Bloom minus the shadow of Odysseus—minus even the shadow of the shadow.

8. Michel de Certeau dedicates his thinking to "the ordinary man," those figures "who lose names and faces as they become the ciphered river of the streets, a mobile language of computations and rationalities that belong to no one ... an Other who is no longer God or the Muse, but the anonymous." He carries on: "The straying of writing outside of its own place is traced by this ordinary man, the metaphor and drift of the doubt which haunts writing, the phantom of its 'vanity,' the enigmatic figure of the relation that writing entertains with all people, with the loss of its exemption, and with its death." This has to do, he tells us, "with democracy, the large city, administrations, cybernetics." On Kawara in a nutshell.

9. Who's writing, though? On Kawara himself writes very little; almost nothing. Whenever he can, he outsources the actual act of writing—of taking up a pen and scribbling down words—to a telegraph clerk, or an adjustable rubber stamp. Or to those giant adjustable rubber stamps, the printing presses. "Two students shot in Santo Domingo." "65 people in Harlem for Malcolm X." "The fire of Mineola Hotel." "The killer of Wendy Sue Wolin, 7, is still hiding somewhere." Stories, each of which would fuel a nineteenth-century novel, become, in the uniformity of their appearance, the endlessness of their procession, repetitive and monotonous as well, flattened down to a neutral, rolling screed of race riots, assassinations, royal visits, civil wars, devaluations, massings of refugees, hijackings, arms deals, uranium-enriching treaties, tenement fires, troop movements, hurricanes, more arms deals, prison riots, currency flotations, earthquakes, air disasters—and (yes) kidnappings. "The Brazilian Government agreed today to a second demand by the kidnappers of the Japanese consul general, Nobuo Okuchi, and said his safety was now in the hands of his captors." "Argentine guerillas kidnapped the British honorary consul in Rosario, Stanley M. Sylvester, today and said he would be 'tried before a people's court of justice.'" The world is writing itself, already, all the time.

10. January 23, 1970: "A death mask stolen, of James Joyce."

11. De Certeau talks about "scriptural systems." Just like Kafka's prisoners, we're stuck inside a giant writing machine (the main feature of Kafka's one is the incising "harrow"—so the term *harrowing* is voided of emotional implications, denoting instead simply the action of groove cutting, of mark making). These systems are another name for power, for control. It's not so much that language is political; rather, the other way around: politics is a linguistic issue. "Users"— that is, consumers, citizens, who play the role of colonized "natives"—make their own paths, their *parole*-acts, through the *langue* of capitalist culture. "Even statistical investigation," writes de Certeau, "remains virtually ignorant of these trajectories, since it is satisfied with classifying, calculating, and putting into tables the 'lexical' units which compose them but to which they cannot be reduced." Elusive, slippery, *parole*-acts are raw, wild, "crazy" even; and the strategy of *langue*, the MO of the Man, is to recuperate these tactics and these moments of subversion, sanitize them, make them "sane" or rational, index and grid them, generally reign them back into the overall scriptural project, the project of power. "What is audible, but far away, will thus be transformed into texts in conformity with the Western desire to read its

products." Is On Kawara parodying this strategy and this desire, this tyrannical mania for making legible? Is he mining the citadel of power with tactical speech-gestures, speech-devices? Or is he just crazy?

12. Perhaps Kawara's a next-generation Félix Fénéon. The midwife of the fin-de-siècle avant-garde was so elusive that his friends called him *L'Homme Invisible, L'Homme qui Silence* (hidden inside that second moniker, The Man Who Silences, is *L'Homme qui s'y Lance*: The Man Who Throws Himself Into It—but what is "it"?). And at the same time he was everywhere: man about town, perpetually drifting down the boulevards, hanging around the cafés ("I Met…"), as he amassed his copy for *La Revue Blanche*—the White, or Blank, Review. Fénéon invented, in *Le Figaro*, the three-line news-haiku. "It was his turn at nine-pins when a cerebral hemorrhage felled M. André, seventy-five, of Levallois. While his ball was rolling, he ceased to be." He once left a bomb on the windowsill of a café that was frequented by diplomats and bankers. It went off while he sipped an absinthe at another café round the corner (his route, on that day as on any other, would, if marked, have looked just like an On Kawara map). Arraigned and put on trial, he called, as a character witness, (who else?) Mallarmé: pioneer of blank space, her-

ald of the end of narrative, of figuration, of all art—its end, or rather its overhaul into the always in-progress or to-come project that he (Mallarmé) would simply call The Book. Fénéon, despite his self-evident guilt, was acquitted. He claimed that the explosives found in his writing desk were for stunning fish.

13. De Certeau talks about the practice of *perruque. Perruque* is when the little guy, the worker, does something for his own ends under the guise of obediently serving his employer. When a cabinetmaker uses a lathe to make a piece of furniture for his living room, that's *perruque*; so is when a market researcher or ad-agency employee abandons himself to reverie for half an hour. Whacking off on the boss's time. Or going fly fishing. What *perruque* pilfers, or reclaims, is not material or funds, but simply time. De Certeau links this tactic to invention, and to ethics, and to art. To bring *perruque* to bear upon the everyday, he writes—to do this *in the form of* writing—"would be to practice an 'ordinary' art, to find oneself in the common situation, and to make a kind of *perruque* of writing itself."

14. Ten years, that is, 3,650 or so days, ago, I took part in an iteration of Kawara's ongoing performance piece *One Million Years*. I sat inside a glass box in Trafalgar Square and read the years out, one by one, into a microphone. 48896 BC 48894 BC 51700 AD 51702 AD. I read alternate years, since On Kawara had decreed that one man and one woman should sit in the box, side by side, speaking the dates in turns, like newsreaders. It lasted for a week, around the clock, with teams reading in relay, two-hour stints. I took the morning slot: at about 10 a.m. I'd report to a room (I don't recall the number) in a swish hotel (I don't recall the name) just off the square. Each morning, when I got there, I would be regaled by stories of the night before. These tales were never firsthand: the dead-of-night-shift readers would be long in bed by now. Nor were they even secondhand, since their relief-shift would have finished hours ago as well. The stories were like Chinese whispers, urban myths started that very day, Today: about nightclubbers throwing kebabs at the box; drunk girls flashing their breasts; boys pissing against the glass...

15. He wants you to read it soberly, reflectively, we were told. How will we know if we're doing it right? I wondered out loud. He'll be watching, one of the other volunteers said. You think so? I asked. Yeah, he answered: read it too fast, or frivolously, and this mad old Japanese guy will pop up from the crowd and shout: *You done it wrong!* I tried to remain neutral and indifferent. When I got to the years that ended 1970, 1972, 1974, and so on, though, this became difficult. Although the numbers had at least one other digit at their front, they still recalled for me the 1970s, when I'd been a small child: 1972 was when my brother was born; '75 my sister. So I'd see these little babies, and their lives, what they'd become, all set against the savagery of dinosaurs, the mineral indifference of bubbling, sulfurous pools and meteorites, the brutal amnesia of eons. Nabokov: "the dreadful pitfalls of eternity, the unknowledgeable beyond the unknown, the helplessness, the cold."

16. *Perruque.* One morning, bored of the stale croissants and bad coffee that the Arts Council or Zwirner Gallery or whoever it was organizing the whole operation were serving up in the room, I went down to the hotel's five-star restaurant and ordered a full breakfast. It was great. When the waiter brought me the bill, I wrote down the room number; but

he asked me for a name as well. It's not under my name, I told him; maybe the Arts Council, Zwirner.... But we need a person's name, he said, politely but insistently. I thought for a while, then signed it: On Kawara.

17. To say *I Am Still Alive* is, ultimately, banal. To state *I Am Dead*, though: to be able to say that and mean it, to affirm its truth—that would be something else, something amazing. Blanchot describes facing a firing squad as a young man during the war, and, at the final moment, as the soldiers raised their guns and aimed, feeling exhilaration at the thought of fully experiencing the instant of his death, of both being possessed by and possessing it, living its time as present and as presence—and goes on to describe his enormous disappointment when, at the last minute, the event failed to happen, and he realized that this consummation had eluded him. He lived to ninety-six, or 34,850 days, forever in the shadow of this moment, this nonmoment, with "the instant of my death henceforth always in abeyance": *l'instant de ma mort désormais toujours en instance.*

18. "To speak one's own death," says de Certeau, would be "to open within the language of interlocution a resurrection that does not restore to life." This opening is not afforded the dying one, he concedes—"and yet," he continues, "my death defines more clearly than anything else what speaking is." He seems to be on the verge of articulating something quite momentous, of performing some great, Lazarus-like miracle of thought and reason—but he pulls away, and shifts his attention back to "the murmuring of everyday practices." These, he says, "do not form pockets in economic society. They have nothing in common with these marginalities that technical organization quickly integrates in order to turn them into signifiers and objects of exchange. On the contrary, it is through them that an uncodable difference insinuates itself into the happy relation the system would like to have with the operations it claims to administer. Far from being a local, and thus classifiable, revolt, it is a common and silent, almost sheeplike subversion—our own." Everyday practices, he concludes, institute their own time: "casual time." And casual time, scattered all along duration, is eternal.

2015

Kathy Acker's Infidel Heteroglossia

As a schoolchild, I had to learn collective nouns for animals: a murder of crows, a bask of crocodiles, a quiver of cobras, an intrusion of cockroaches, and so on. Jellyfish, for some reason, get two of these: *bloom* and *smack*. The first—flowery, Joycean—seems to convey the languid beauty of the seaborne creature whose transparency, paradoxically, enhances rather than diminishes its mystery. The second, guttural and onomatopoeic, instantly conjures up the state in which most humans (those of us who aren't marine biologists) actually encounter these cnidarians: as mucilaginous patches splatted on the beach alongside other refuse; frayed smudges marking the sea's fringe hem; lumpen offerings for cruel children to poke and pick up at the end of sticks before, curiosity sated, flinging against rocks.

Dickens's Thames may not have any jellyfish in it, but Kathy Acker's "plagiarized" *Great Expectations* is awash with them. "My mother," writes its narrator O, "is a dummy and a piece of jellyfish. The most disgusting thing in this world is her. My worst nightmare is that I'll have some of that jellyfish in me." A few pages later, we are told that "the jellyfish is the rapist"; later still, we get an actual nightmare in which "a huge jellyfish glop who's shaped into an-at-least-six-story worm is chasing her down the main sand-filled cowboy street. All of her WANTS to get away, but her body isn't obeying her mind." Yet later, O's body "becomes" her father's (that is, the rapist's) desire, and jellyfish, collectively, express their own desire to become O; which leads, by a process of psycho-gelatinous osmosis, to O contracting an ovarian infection.

Acker—like Joyce, like Kafka—is a hardcore materialist. "One could say," she writes in *My Death My Life by Pier Paolo Pasolini*, plagiarizing the magnificent climax of Flaubert's *The Temptation of Saint Anthony*, "that he seeks to merge with unnameable nature, fleeing the weight of nomination in the unnameable texture of things, I want people to treat me as an animal, in the irregular indefinable movements of the foliage, of the waves. To be matter." In *Empire of the Senseless*, as Freud's case-histories receive her plagiarism treatment (which in fact is very singular: an Acker plagiarism is instantly distinguishable from one by, say, her early mentor Burroughs or her younger admirer Stewart Home), she zooms in on The Wolf Man's mental reduction of God to piles of feces lying in the street, and sees in Schreber's psychosis "the enzyme that could change all my blood." Elsewhere in the same novel, contemplating the back-flow of blood into the syringe of her junky boyfriend, she declares: "My body is open to all people: this is democratic capitalism"; from Pierre Guyotat's *Eden Eden Eden* she steals scenes of soldiers' bodies tearing and entering wounds in those of their colonial victims. In *The Childlike Life of the Black Tarantula by The Black Tarantula* she tells us: "I look at my body as though it were a web, solely a way of asking people to touch me." Open, morphing, endlessly penetrating or being penetrated by the scenes around them, Acker's bodies channel and act as hubs or mainstays in a world of viscerally networked continuity—like jellyfish quivering as pulse-signals reach them through a viscous sea. Or, rather (lest we start getting holistic), they *both* anchor this world *and* serve as its disjecta: more smack than bloom. Janey, the protagonist of *Blood and Guts in High School*, contrasts her body with the "fresh meat" one young girls are meant to have: "Even though I'm younger, I'm tough, rotted, putrid beef. My cunt red ugh." We get a drawing of this organ on the next page, then an account of its growing infected. Abortions crop up frequently throughout the books, semi-repeated in the name of *Empire*'s heroine's companion, Abhor—which

257

taken as a whole, of course, denotes repulsion. *Great Expectations* sees a man invite two friends to have dinner with O "so they could do whatever they want with her in no uncertain terms because she's the most unnameable unthinkable spit spit. She realizes that she is at the same time a little girl absolutely pure nothing wrong just what she wants, and this unnameable dirt this thing. This is not a possible situation. This identity doesn't exist."

Acker might be the first significant novelist to have come of age during the rise within American humanities programs of the set of discourses the latter still rather reductively label "theory." While many of her literary heroes, from Artaud right back to Catullus, furnish ample precedents for the aesthetic of abjection that pervades her writing, its most lucid analytical formulation is found in the work of the critic Julia Kristeva. *Powers of Horror: An Essay on Abjection* received its English publication in 1982, a year before *Great Expectations*, and Acker's indebtedness to Kristeva's thinking has been noted by many critics, and acknowledged by Acker herself. For Kristeva, that which is abjected, thrown away, purged or let drop as waste presents, to the body or system that has ejected it, "one of those violent, dark revolts of being," speaks of an order "beyond the scope of the possible, the tolerable, the thinkable" that "cannot be assimilated." The abject doesn't simply provide an "alternative" point of psychological identification; rather, it "draws me towards a place where meaning collapses," where "consciousness has not assumed its rights and transformed into signifiers those fluid demarcations of yet unstable territories where an 'I' that is taking shape is ceaselessly straying."

This is precisely the quandary, or "impossible situation," Acker's work negotiates: that of identifying with non-identity. Writing under these conditions means foregoing all recourse to "authenticity" or "self-expression" and instead treating any type of subjective iteration—any iteration that affirms or presupposes subjectivity—as provisional, strategic, like a rebel camp to be set up in enemy territory then quickly struck before the powers that be get proper bearings on it. It means accepting (as she writes in *Empire*) that "I, whoever I was going to be, would be a construct"; and accepting exile (as she also states in that book) as a "permanent condition...in terms of relationships and language./ In terms of identity." Reading Kristeva may have helped bring this condition into focus, but it was governing Acker's work right from the off: we see it already in *The Childlike Life*, published almost a decade before *Powers of Horror*, the name and very nature of whose main "character" morph through centuries and across continents, in and out of source texts. "I can see everything in a set of shifting frameworks. I'm interested solely in getting into someone else," this figure tells us. Abjection, claims Kristeva, takes place "when an Other... precedes and possesses me, and through such possessions causes me to be." As the critic Alex Houen points out, for Acker autobiography can only ever be allobiography. While Rimbaud may tell Georges Izambard "*Je est un autre*," and Proust may reverize his way into the books he reads at bedtime, Acker hammers and hacks her way down to a kind of baseline of self-substitution, finishing *The Childlike Life*'s chapters with the words: "All the above events are taken from myself, ENTER MURDERERS! by E. H. Bierstadt, MURDER FOR PROFIT by W. Boitho, BLOOD IN THE PARLOR by D. Dunbar, ROGUES AND ADVENTURESSES by C Kingston," or beginning them: "I MOVE TO SAN FRANCISCO. I BEGIN TO COPY MY FAVOURITE PORNOGRAPHY BOOKS AND BECOME THE MAIN PERSON IN EACH OF THEM."

Kristeva's thought is topographic, almost cartographic, full of territories, frontiers, limits. Drawing from anthropologist Mary Douglas, she claims that "filth is not a quality in itself, but it applies only to what relates to a *boundary* and, more particularly, represents the object jettisoned out of the boundary, its other side, a margin." She suggests of abjection that "we may call it a border"; and she pays careful attention to material micro-borders, membranes such as the shudder-inducing skin that sits atop the surface of a cup of hot milk. What interests her most is when inside and outside start getting confused. Pondering Freud's notion of a "beginning" to mental life that precedes the advent of the word, she writes: "In that anteriority to language, the outside is elaborated by means of a projection from within.... An outside in the image of the inside, made of pleasure and pain." At a certain point in childhood, language, the symbolic order, comes along and differentiates inside and outside; yet, Kristeva adds, "there would be witnesses to the perviousness of the limit, artisans after a fashion who would try to tap that pre-verbal "beginning" within a word that is flush with pleasure and pain." When she names two archetypal artisans of this sort—the primitive and the poet, the latter of whom renders the border permeable through "a recasting of language"—she could more or less be naming Acker's entire project. For Acker, as for Douglas, disgustingness has no aesthetic value of its own. "I'm not trying to tell you about the rotgut weird parts of my life," she writes in *Blood and Guts*. "Abortions are the symbol, the outer image, of sexual relations in the world. Describing my abortions is the only real way I can tell you about pain and fear... my unstoppable drive for sexual love made me know." The body's castaway, an unformed fetus, held up to the light by the act of being narrated, reveals the leakiness of the border between inside and outside, public and private, morality and law and the host of other categories that make up the social order. Or, to be precise, the *sexual* body's castaway brings this about. Sex is the prime zone where these things overlap, where limits might be crossed, through excess and perversion. As *Empire*, breaking into verse, states: "Sex is public: the streets made themselves for us to walk naked down them take out your cock and piss over me. / The threshold is there.... Go over this threshold with me."

II.

A recurrent motif in Acker's novels is that of the prisoner—a figure whom the outside world keeps locked away "inside." If Acker has read her Kristeva, she has also read her Foucault, for whom prison—in its architecture, codes and rituals— serves as a perfect model for the overall regimes of power and control governing "free" society. "We live in prison," Acker writes in *Blood and Guts*. "Most of us don't know we live in prison." But even closer to her thinking on this theme than Foucault's is that of Giorgio Agamben, the Italian phi- losopher most of whose work (or its translation into En- glish) Acker's writing, far from plagiarizing, uncannily and almost to a *t* anticipates. Agamben, too, is fascinated by borders and thresholds, by the liminal experience of "be- ing-*within* and *outside*," by the abjection of the things held in the no-man's-land of limbo. These "things" include, historically, deceased unbaptized children (the abortion's close relation), refugees held in transit zones and prisoners. Digging up an ancient Roman statute that designated a certain class of criminal as *homo sacer*—"sacred man" whom, being beyond the law, it was perfectly legal for anyone to kill but who, being sacred, could not be used in ceremonial or ritual sacrifice—Agamben sees in the "living dead man" that this double- or counter-law (a law through which law itself is suspended) produced a precedent for subjects living under the "state of exception" in which modern tyrannies (which, for him, would already include the hyper-securitized neoliberalism we've lived through for the last few decades, never mind the quasi-fascist order we appear to currently be entering) are grounded. Acker's prisoners are exact embodiments of *homo sacer*: "The fact is," she writes in *Empire*, "that all prisoners should be killed by the state and, since they haven't been, they're in actuality beyond death./ Thus, prisoners are sacred. Their lives are imaginary, *imaginary* as in "imaginary number," not rationally possible."

What's most interesting from a literary point of view is that this slippery limit, this porous limbo-zone in which inside and outside, law and lawlessness, life and death all hang suspended, is the very territory Acker designates as the place where writing, as a material act, originates. What, she asks, customarily marks out prisoners even—especially—when they've stripped their uniforms off? Tattoos. (An observation that dates her: tattoos have now become so thoroughly middle- and even upper-class that the Canadian prime minister and the wife of a recent British one sport them.) Tattoos not only (traditionally) proliferate on the social threshold that is prison; they also flood and impregnate the corporal threshold, the shuddery top-film, of human skin. Acker, herself extensively tattooed, devotes whole passages of *Empire* (a book she dedicates "to my tattooist") to describing how the surface of the skin is raised to make tattoos. She also points out that, in Tahitian, "ta-tau" means, simply, "writing." The passage in which her character Agone receives his prison-tattoo is uncharacteristically subtle in its plagiarism; but one source, lurking behind references to Pacific island customs, must surely be Melville's Queequeg, *Moby-Dick*'s harpoonist whose own Polynesian body is entirely covered in tattoos that map the earth and heavens, the horizons round which life and death are hinged. Agone's tattoo depicts a ship:

> The first color was red. The first color was blood. The ship's sails were crimson. Blood makes the body move. Blood made the ship's body move. Blood changed the inhuman winds into human breath. Agone sang with the

pain. The crimson streams of the winds were the roses surrounding the ship.

The second color was brown. Brown is the color of excreted blood or shit. The ship was flying on its human-made wings in harmony with the elements: blue sea, blue sky. The earth, home, nations are the sailor's enemy, end to his journey, his death. The brown of the ship's body reminds the sailor that his journey must end in death.

Queequeg's death, we should recall, is both imprecise and substituted: having first contracted a fever that convinces him he'll die, and had a coffin built for him by the ship's carpenter, he makes a complete recovery; after which he whiles away the time transcribing his tattoos from his body to the outer surface of the coffin which is—for now and for him at least—redundant. When the *Pequod* sinks and he does die, it's Ishmael who'll float on the coffin back to safety: the crafted box becomes the craft, or life raft, that conveys the narrative to us. In both *Moby-Dick* and *Empire*, the tattoo, its crafting, serves as miniature or *mise-en-abîme* of the book itself, and of the practice of text-generation. "The most positive thing in the book," claims Acker in an interview, "is the tattoo. It concerns taking over, doing your own sign-making."

If, Queequeg aside, Acker wears her influences not so much on her sleeve as scrawled over her skin, then there's one prisoner who occupies a prime spot on her literary *corpus*: Sade. History's most famous, or infamous, prison-writer, imprisoned *for* the act of writing on a body (he'd scored marks in the flesh of a prostitute and poured wax—another writing-surface or substance—into these), Sade wrote at the very spot where tyranny, revolution and terror came to share a border: the Bastille. One version of the prison sacking holds that it was Sade himself who sparked it, by using his open ended (and presumably feces-stained) chamber pot as a trumpet and announcing to the crowds massed outside that the warders had begun executing prisoners (which they hadn't). Another tells that the leaders of the mob who sacked the Bastille, searching for instruments of torture to display as evidence of the ancien regime's cruelty, found only a confiscated printing press—and, figuring that the largely illiterate crowd wouldn't know any different, held it up on view as just one such contraption. Sade provides Acker with her greatest and most monumental template for the interiorization of a political exterior, and vice versa: "I've remade the outside prison inside me," she has him (or is it the other way round?) say in *The Childlike Life*, "because there's no difference between outside and inside my mind: they release me from prison and I'm still in prison." This ventriloquized statement is swiftly followed by a kind of literary manifesto: "I'm trying to get away from self-expression but not from personal life. I hate creativity. I'm simply exploring other ways of dealing with events than ways my lousy habits— mainly installed by parents and institutions—have forced me to act."

The conjunction of these passages is telling. One might think that the obvious point of overlap between Acker and Sade lies in the erotic excess both their writing enacts—and, to be sure, that's there. But, while his name has lent itself to a whole personality-type, very few people have actually *read* Sade. The directory-size *One Hundred and Twenty Days of Sodom* strikes me, above all, as a giant manual not so much of sex as of a certain mode of *narrative*. The set-up for the extended program of depravities in which Sade's four libertine protagonists engage involves a modification of the Chateau de Silling's hall into a "salon" with a main floor and four corner-niches ("recesses," Sade calls them). In the center of the floor, four seasoned prostitutes hold forth in relay, one at time, recounting their most lewd and debauched sexual escapades to the libertines, while a pool of sixteen kidnapped children (eight of each gender) on the cusp of puberty sit at their feet. The libertines occupy the salon's corners, one in each niche. The "game-rules" stipulate that, at any point, the libertines (and only they) may interrupt the prostitutes' stories in order to reenact and (through a set of almost algorithmic corporeal variations) modify them, using the teens as "extras" to this end. Sade is very dogmatic about this governing commandment; he even writes a note reminding himself of it: "Never have the four friends do anything until it has first been recounted." What's being dramatized here, then, is what we might call a "space of narrative." The prostitutes' second-hand tales provide this space's starting content; while the space's terms or "settings" afford (to some) the option of switching from being a passive listener (or "reader") into an active doer (or re-doer)—which switch, in turn, involves an act of violence.

This narrative regime—we could say, this regime of narrative—is structurally similar to the one within which Acker's violence-saturated retellings take place. The plagiarism in which she sets so much stock isn't just a style or gimmick. In its systematic assault on originality, that sacred fetish to which (alongside authenticity and self-expression) middlebrow fiction and its teaching still pay constant homage; in its induction of a mode of "second-hand-ness" no less pervasive than Sade's; its obedience to a dictum of never having anything enacted that is not a reenactment, remix or permutation of a source found in some other archive—it affirms at every level a belief that the artist (poet, novelist) is operating with materials and within frames that are neither of her own making, nor politically neutral; ones that require aggressive—that is, violent—reconfiguration. Sitting (as friends describe) cross-legged on the floor each time she first reads a text by one of the "greats," furiously hammering at her typewriter to rework it, is for Acker not simply a form of apprenticeship, but rather a strategy unleashed both with and against an entire cultural edifice. The great paradox is that while middlebrow fiction, endlessly recycling tired humanist clichés under the guise of originality, is in truth profoundly unoriginal, Acker's unabashed re-working of old stock—like the appropriations and *détournements* carried out by Lettrists and Situationists two decades before her, or the pictorial and sculptural reproductions of her contemporary Sherrie Levine (an artist for whom she expressed much admiration)—genuinely unleashes fresh, dynamic cultural potential.

III.

These practices—citation, reenactment, *repetitio* and modification-through-repetition—already of course, in one way or other, have their place right at the heart of the Western canon (there'd be no Shakespeare without them). But intriguingly, Acker finds her most important precedent for them not in the European but rather in the Arabic toolbox.

"Arabs (in their culture) have no (concept of) originality," she tells us in *Don Quixote*. "They write by cutting chunks out of all-ready written texts and in other ways defacing traditions: changing important names into silly ones, making dirty jokes out of matters that should be of the utmost importance to us such as nuclear warfare." Accordingly, her rewrites are earnest in their frivolousness and vice versa. "What time tomorrow will we be able to fuck?" asks the Juliet of *My Death My Life*. "As soon as the morning sun has shot its sperm over all blackness and the Wall Street lawyer is masturbating in his office," replies Romeo. The Arabic, or rather Arabian, influence is written all over *Empire* too. "This is true. Oh Sultan of Reality," the narrative voice interjects at one point, invoking Scheherazade, that figure for whom violence and recounting are most intimately conjoined (if she stops narrating she'll be beheaded). In *Blood and Guts* Janey learns Persian writing, a "language/to get rid of language"; she is also "formed" or educated by a Persian slave-trader, before attaching herself in Tangier to her near namesake Jean Genet, Sade's twentieth-century prison-writer counterpart, himself politically and personally invested in the Arabic world, who makes a cameo appearance in the book. *Empire*, which contains sections titled "In Honor of the Arabs," "Let the Algerians Take Over Paris" and "On Becoming Algerian," is also steeped in direct references to Arab uprisings against European masters, and subsequent brutal police clampdowns. If Arabic or Middle Eastern culture provides a signpost pointing to a form of writing that avoids or negates the "creativity" she so despises, the Arabic human figure, especially in its role of colonial subject who's become rebellious, furnishes Acker with, if not a straightforward point of identification, then a multi-faceted cluster whose collective outline suggests possibilities of subversive agency. Inspired by their Arab counterparts, *Empire*'s American rebels, the "modern Terrorists," launch an all-out assault on the techno-capitalist "central control network," ringed with satellite and radio connections, known as MAINLINE, into whose internal video-feed they "shoot misinformation" in a (classically Burroughsian) attempt to bring the whole caboodle—corporate power, the state, media, the entire symbolic order—crashing down.

If empire is technocratic, then colonial bodies (that is, all bodies, since empire is a general condition) are a space of technological mastery, like robots operated by remote control. Not for nothing is Abhor described in *Empire*'s first sentence as "part robot, and part black." In Acker's general mythography, wetware and software merge: the body, as a site of power, is *de facto* a site of systematic and machinic intervention—or, to give such intervention its late-twentieth-century name, code. It's code the modern

Terrorists have raided MAINLINE for, and coded subprograms they use to raid it. Code is not only what's written on the body: it's what writes the body in the first place. We are all robots. The revolutionary act would not be to "rescue" an imagined "natural" body *from* technology, but rather to take over the technology itself, remake its program. Here, Acker's thought dovetails with that of Donna Haraway, who writes in "A Cyborg Manifesto" (first published in 1985, three years before *Empire*) that "communications sciences and modern biologies are constructed by a common move— *the translation of the world into a problem of coding*, a search for a common language in which all resistance to instrumental control disappears." Against this specter Haraway proposes not a luddite but a "cyborg politics," which would be a "struggle for language and the struggle against perfect communication, against the one code that translates all meaning perfectly, the central dogma of phallogocentrism." For Haraway as for Acker, rebellion, as a techno-linguistic act, is inseparable from the understanding of gender as a means of coding and controlling bodies. A cyborg uprising would involve bodies entering (to borrow Ovid's phrase) "a state of mutation" in order to subvert their codings, write themselves anew. Citing salamanders who grow duplicated, if deformed, new limbs where old ones have been amputated, Haraway claims: "We have all been injured, profoundly. We require regeneration, not rebirth, and the possibilities for our reconstitution include the utopian dream of the hope for a monstrous world without gender." The "cyborg imagery" that would help generate this regenerated, monstrous world, she argues (turning, like Acker, to terminology that carries strong Arabic or Islamic overtones), "is a dream not of a common language, but of a powerful infidel heteroglossia." Those last four words (librarians take note) would constitute a fitting catalog description of Acker's oeuvre.

When Janey's learning Persian writing, she immerses herself simultaneously in *The Scarlet Letter*, Hawthorne's landmark parable of gender politics and bodies with inscriptions on them. "At this point in *The Scarlet Letter* and in my life," she writes, "politics don't disappear but take place inside my body." For Kristeva, the abject is not only (to use a term she shares with Haraway) monstrous, but also delirious, rhapsodic, "*something added* that expands us, overstrains us, and causes us to be both *here*, as dejects, and *there*, as others and sparkling. A divergence, an impossible bounding. Everything missed, joy—fascination." Acker, whose life was cut short by her own body's mutation in the form of breast cancer (coupled with a techno-capitalist regime that meant her health insurance didn't meet the cost of treatment that would have saved her), seemed to share Kristeva's sentiment—and to sense that it would (as befits the allobiographical logic running through her work) be some-one else, or several someone elses, not she, who saw this divergent fascination through. Janey, speaking as Hawthorne's Hester for Acker—or Hester speaking as Hawthorne's Acker for Janey, or any combination of the above—speculates: "There's going to be a world where the imagination is created by joy not suffering, a man and a woman can love each other again they can kiss and fuck again (a woman's going to come along and make this world for me even though I'm not alive anymore)." It might just be that the final measure of a writer is not so much what they achieve themselves as what they render possible for others.

2016

Sources

The essays in this book were originally published or presented as follows:

"Meteomedia, or Why London's Weather Is in the Middle of Everything" was published in *London from Punk to Blair*, edited by Joe Kerr and Andrew Gibson (London: Reaktion Press, 2003).

"Why *Ulysses* Matters" was delivered as a lecture at the University of Chicago in 2013 and published under the title "*Ulysses* and Its Wake" in the *London Review of Books* (June 19, 2014).

"Kool Thing, or Why I Want to Fuck Patty Hearst" was published in *The Empty Page: Fiction Inspired by Sonic Youth*, edited by Peter Wild (London: Serpent's Tale, 2008), which was published in the United States as *Noise: Fiction Inspired by Sonic Youth*, edited by Peter Wild (New York: Harper Perennial, 2009).

"Get Real, or What Jellyfish Have to Tell Us About Literature" was published under the title "Writing Machines" in the *London Review of Books* (December 18, 2014).

"*Tristram Shandy*: On Balls and Planes" was published as the introduction to Laurence Sterne, *Tristram Shandy* (New York: Vintage, 2013).

"Recessional, or the Time of the Hammer" was delivered as a lecture at the Cabaret Voltaire, Zurich, in 2015, then published as *Recessional— Or, the Time of the Hammer* (Chicago: Diaphanes Press, 2016).

"Blurring the Sublime: On Gerhard Richter" was published under the title "Blurred Visionary: Gerhard Richter's Photo-Paintings" in *The Guardian* (September 22, 2011).

"The Prosthetic Imagination of David Lynch" was delivered as a lecture at Tate Modern, London, in 2009, and published in slightly different form as "His Dark Materials" in the *New Statesman* (January 8, 2010).

"From Feedback to Reflux: Kafka's Cybernetics of Revolt" was published as the introduction to Franz Kafka, *Letter to His Father*, translated by Ernst Kaiser and Eithne Wilkins (New York: Vintage, 2015).

"The Geometry of the Pressant" was published as the introduction to Alain Robbe-Grillet, *Jealousy*, translated by Richard Howard (Richmond, UK: Alma Books, 2008), and reprinted in *Artforum* (Summer 2008).

"Stabbing the Olive: Jean-Philippe Toussaint" was published in the *London Review of Books* (February 11, 2010).

"On Dodgem Jockeys" was first broadcast on the BBC radio program *The Verb* (September 23, 2011), then published in *The Believer* (May 2012).

"Nothing Will Have Taken Place Except the Place" was delivered as a lecture at the Royal College of Art, London, and at Notre Dame University, Indiana, in 2015.

"18 Semiconnected Thoughts on Michel de Certeau, On Kawara, Fly Fishing, and Various Other Things" was published in *On Kawara—Silence*, the catalogue accompanying the Guggenheim exhibit of the same name at the Solomon R. Guggenheim Museum, New York, in 2015.

"Kathy Acker's Infidel Heteroglossia" was delivered as a lecture at the Center for Fiction, New York, May 9, 2017.

Tom McCarthy's work has been translated into more than twenty languages. His previous books include *Remainder*, *C*, *Satin Island*, and *Tintin and the Secret of Literature*. He is the founder and general secretary of the International Necronautical Society (INS), a semi-fictitious avant-garde network. In 2013 he was awarded the inaugural Windham-Campbell Prize for Fiction by Yale University. He lives in London.